THE OTHER SIDE OF LANDSCAPE
AN ANTHOLOGY OF CONTEMPORARY NORDIC POETRY

THE OTHER SIDE OF LANDSCAPE
AN ANTHOLOGY OF CONTEMPORARY NORDIC POETRY

EDITED BY ANNI SUMARI
& NICOLAJ STOCHHOLM

SLOPE EDITIONS
NEW YORK | NEW HAMPSHIRE | MASSACHUSETTS

Published by Slope Editions
www.slopeeditions.org

Library of Congress Cataloging-in-Publication Data
The other side of landscape : an anthology of contemporary Nordic poetry /
edited by Anni Sumari & Nicolaj Stochholm.— 1st ed.
     p. cm.
   ISBN 0-9718219-8-4 (alk. paper)
   1. Scandinavian poetry--20th century--Translations into English. 2.
Finnish poetry—20th century—Translations into English. I. Sumari, Anni,
1965- II. Stochholm, Nicolaj.

PT7093.O67 2006
839'.5—dc22

2006002602

Photograph & Cover Design by Jonathan Link
Text set is Sabon, Display set in Minion

Printed in the United States of America
9 8 7 6 5 4 3 2 1
FIRST EDITION

Thanks to the Editors of *Circumference* and *Rattapallax* for publishing some of the poems that appear in this anthology.

Thanks to all the generous sponsors who made this book possible: The Nordic Culture Fund, Norwegian Literature Abroad (NORLA), Kolon Publishers, The Danish Art Council, The Finnish Literature Information Centre (FILI), The Swedish Institute

Nordic Culture Fund

Swedish Institute

Contents

Nicolaj Stochholm (continued)

Lars Skinnebach
translated by Barbara Haveland

~ Iceland ~

Didda (Sigurlaug Jónsdóttir)
translated by the poet
with Bernard Scudder & Gordon Whalmsley

~ Sweden ~

~ NORWAY ~

PUBLISHER'S NOTE

Slope Editions is honored to have worked with Anni Sumari and Nicolaj Stochholm, who strove tirelessly to realize their vision: the anthology in your hands. It's full of great, varied pieces. In bringing these poems from across the world into the US, the poets, translators, and editors help us to see their world and our own world anew.

Refracted through cultures not-quite-our-own, these voices come as otherworldly. Not only are we given glimpses of what is seen, heard, and tasted beyond our borders but we also feel instructed. A Nordic aesthetic, a Nordic history, a Nordic poetry teach new and delicious techniques for seeing, hearing, and tasting. It's a confrontation of sorts. We see ourselves and our own lands from a different vantage point, from a new and wonderfully peculiar landscape.

—*Christopher Janke*
Turners Falls, Massachusetts
December 20, 2005

Just to Write it Anew

This anthology is a short glimpse into the variety and abundance of new Nordic poetry — just as every poem is a short glimpse into the life that's created by minds themselves, minds which keep this blue earthly rock in circulation around the sun — it's a glimpse into a life simply moving: yes, we are here, with an open five-fingered desire, with a fistful of immortality.

Electrical I, electrical town, electrical hey-hey, electrical moon, electrical bridge, electrical memory, electrical letter, electrical light, electrical spring, electrical screen, electrical eye. Everything concerning the I can be called romantic; modernism and postmodernism are evolving from and elaborating on the heritage of the mighty eye; they are liberated from traditional sails. In this spirit, our selections salute the different parts of our shared consciousness in their plentitude and richness of possibility, and as the celebration of the vastness within every single life. We acknowledge that our choice of poets for this anthology is highly personal. It is based on much careful reading and passionate dialogue.

Nordic poetry is deeply influenced both by American and Central European poetry, and by its own co-existence with 1000 year-old fragments hammered in stone or painted on dried leather. These ancient texts include the body of literature known as the Edda, which derives from pan-Scandinavian mythology and includes among its best-known epics the Icelanders' sagas; and Kalevala, the Finnish national epic, with its unique cosmology and heroic tales. The New Nordic poetry we present in this book is an amalgam of present and past, foreign and indigenous. We have long ago stopped branding our Nordic light. It's just here — miraculously — born again over the local 7-Eleven and Arab kiosk in the new blazing dawn.

Our most heartfelt thanks to everyone involved in the making of this book, from the various national and Nordic cultural institutions whose grants made it possible for the translators to do their work, to the translators themselves, to the good people at Slope Editions: Chris Janke, Ethan Paquin, and those many others there who worked together to make this anthology come together. We would like to extend our warmest thanks to Matthew Zapruder, who first introduced us and our idea for this anthology to Chris and Ethan.

—Anni Sumari and Nicolaj Stochholm
Helsinki and Copenhagen, December 2005

MORTEN SØNDERGAARD

~

DENMARK
TRANSLATED BY JOHN IRONS

LANDSCAPES

To.
To walk.
To walk backwards in one's tracks.
Step: Name.
Walk: Movable names.
You asked me if I felt like going for a walk,
        and the question
branched out into the landscape.
The landscape tries out a voice on us,
        it tries to pronounce
our unfamiliar names,
but we are also unable
to formulate it. What do you want to know?
It says: "Don't be afraid. Stay."
        We say: "We are already here."
The apple trees blossom self-evidently
and teach us to see with words.

The second landscape.
        Again: Words are doors that are ajar.
You had a blossoming apple branch with you for me.
At times the swallows make a
mistake and fly around inside the house.
This bustle. Guests phone to say
        they are on their way.
We go for a walk from a swallow's eye view. In their eyes

we are lit-up enigmas.
They make clamorous comments about us:
"Ma, come si fa?" The swallows do not walk on the ground.
They maneuver in the air. The mountains and trees stand still,
      I move
in relation to them. A figure on a background
with no reverse. The swallows daub my eyes
      shut with wet clay
and real images.

The guests have arrived.
One cannot help seeing
a demented god revealing himself
in their looks when they knock on the door
      and talk excitedly
with each other on their mobile phones.
They want to be fetched at distant stations,
but when I bring out their suitcases,
they want nothing to do with them, and their gifts haven't
      been wrapped.
We were woken in the middle of the night
by a cloudburst. The landscape read us
      like an open book. Afterwards everything
smelled of warm earth and wet grass, but we were too
shy to attribute any meaning to that.

To say: Everything. The same thing as saying: Walk.
To say: Walk. The same thing as saying: Let
      the landscape walk through you. To say: Landscape.
The same thing as saying: Everything. Walk backwards,
that is the gesture of the painter, and immediately
the landscape poses, as if it were
      about to be painted, and not the
Mona Lisa, La Gioconda.
The landscape tugs at us like a child that is bored,

it is only held up by the horizon drones of the cicadas.
Step into the house. Step in through the frame.
        The same thing as saying: Step into the landscape.
I collect everything-I-know in small stacks
and set them on fire.

Death writes and writes.
Today the talking olive tree came over to me and said:
"Life is a transition from nothing to
        nothing."
But you can't say something like that
to anybody? The landscape unfolds outwards like
the pages of a book. *Ein Nervenreiz. Un état d'âme.*
        We have understood nothing. And that's that.
What's between the lines of the landscape
is impossible to read. We unfurl the full stops
        into stars, and the guests return from
their evening walk with panic-stricken eyes and their clothes
spattered with wine.

The landscape inside the house. It's raining.
        But it's not raining. Most things are true.
The guests want to have breakfast in bed.
In the midst of the living grass.
The ants transport
landscapes of widely differing origins
        round amongst themselves.
The ants place them in a heap
        and the landscapes become one.
Display the utmost caution when dealing with
landscapes. The continents migrate. We make love
        like curious children, and the apple trees
have lost their blossom.

Oh lay off! These stairs of flesh
that give way at each step
       and lead directly up into theoretical superstructures on
economy
and the sexuality of dead authors.
The stupid analysis creaks somewhat.
       All it amounts to is saying
that chance is competing with death
to arrive first at the brains of the new-born.
I am unfinished, a crank of steel bearings
that rattle across the marble floor, the guests' voices
       invade me and blah blah blah

To. This: To.
One cannot say: "Turn left at the big tree,"
for the sentence does not quite reach it.
Now the guests want a late snack. They are arguing about
       who is to sleep where.
The gaze runs and runs, stretches out, dashes back
and forth across the same incomprehensible line.
But the landscape is unreadable,
       and we cast
skeletal shadows. Come, let's go for a walk instead.
We walk through doors of a certain size.
The doors shut and open. Read: The size of the doors
       is determined by that of the humans.
In the landscape the doors are designed for gods.

13 December: St Lucia's Day.
We lead a woman into the church, she is bearing
her eyes on a small platter.
       But the age of miracles is past.
Inside close by stands a meteorologist
in his rubber cell of a TV studio
promising good weather for the next couple of weeks.

We do not interfere,
        it feels simply embarrassing
with all the stock exchange figures and computer graphics.
Each poem lights up its piece of the world with its torch.
it is a way of making it precise.
        Dear,
We are two synchronous watches,
going with our separate lives.
We take turns carrying each other
like tired children. Finally we fall into words,
        continue our separate flesh-letters to the wind.
With my finger tips I made sure
        that you make sense even so.
Love,

I translated what you had said,
but left out the
most important thing.
Come, let's change into trees!
Grow. Put out new leaves and shoots.
The swallows glide
        through the garden air
like soundless scalpels.
The fireflies sew the sky together with shining stitches.
The landscape put indiscreet questions.
But we cannot utter a word, the sentences
        grow gnarled like old trees:
We have to keep the most important thing to ourselves.

The moon above the valley, in flight.
We do not dare sleep, it is burning so brightly.
        The landscape moves in. It is looking for something
edible. The guests arrive: I thought it was you.
The guests leave: it was you.
        It is us, there are guests, immigrants
that keep on walking. If we only got down to it

a little more realistically, we would already be there.
      The green lounge suit of the vines
flutters on the hillsides.
      Better look the other way,
for the houses are out and about on the roads, they have
left their foundations. Departures everywhere.
The places invade us, and defenseless we allow ourselves
      to be led nowhere. We could settle here. We.

One tries again with a desperate mouth,

but it cannot be done. Perhaps
it is the words
      that say us.
Move on. The swallows chatter.
Attention caught
by what is apparently irrelevant:
      Here everyone has access.
The guests merge with the view.
They screw. And the apple trees have other business.
I leave myself like a house:
      The I-landscape.
Sorry. That wasn't what I meant.
It ought to have been different.
More honest. But that was impossible.

As you were!
I'm well aware that the landscape tries to imagine
us with the big scarecrows
on the hilltop. The blind cat
      stalks in the secret garden.
Scarecrows, hills, trees, fields of sunflowers
come up close and scrutinize our faces.
But the landscape lies beyond every meaning.
It thinks its own thoughts. On the other hand:

We are trees with legs.
We cannot stay here. Come, let's walk.
Let's walk the thought-plank.

Due to my poor sense of direction
        I have got lost, but, all things considered,
that's of minor importance. In a moment I will walk
"over there." Before, I was "here." Right now I am a place
        between "there" and "here."
The ants lug off the landscape,
grains of sugar between working mandibles,
bit by bit. But the ants themselves are bits
linked by an enormous association.
        Don't look at me like that! I'm only trying
to say things straight as they are. The Shouter shouts "Sirocco,"
and fine sand from the Sahara covers every surface.

Once again: That was not the way it was meant to be.
Send me more ultramarine, for the landscape is
congealed noise. There is so much else that has to
be said before it is too late.
It just keeps on,
        it grows
like grass and mold on each and every surface.
Ivy hands are handed in across a wall.
Spring's machine is self-operating.
The wind sighs in the olive trees. A noise of nothing.
Have we neglected some opportunity?
        Let's eat off the ugly white bone plates tonight.
I put out a bowl of milk for the blind cat.
The world fell apart and was put together again
        by the intelligent child.

A wildly lit ferry out of control
        plows through the landscape.

I did not know it had been docked
inside the house, but it is New Year's Eve,
and the guests have cut the moorings.
        Let go! We are refugees hanging over the railings
on the boat of chance. Keep going,
for there is nothing else than poems
        and a cluttered everyday to pit against
the evil and dizzying groove of time.
I say: I love each deadening beat
        of your heart. You say: it is as if I
was you. But you are not to be afraid.
        For you are, and the poem stands
laughing like an old transistor
into the chaos of twilight.

Words: Their number increases as I use them.
The swallows fly around with them in their beaks.
        They hang in the grass, they stick to the stinging
nettles.
What we are: A gray powder mixed up with the clouds.
What we are not: Landscape. This more: Sideways, sideways.
        It continues beyond the frame. A song
someone keeps on humming.
We move from right to left. Mirror-writing.
The guests call for coffee and send e-mails.
Their voices fill the whole house. At night
chaos rents the sealed room.
During the day the bat sleeps from the roof of the poem.
        I go downstairs to chop firewood. The axe is
ready in the chopping-block.

From, the far side of the landscape a dog can be heard
confirming uninvited that the world exists.
        A chainsaw. Voices. A bell. The swallows.
A silver spider runs back and forth,

defining all the contours. There are nightingales
        that sing during the daytime, madly,
because they have
forgotten to dream. The snakes mate on
the paths. The sun does not move.
Perhaps it will all be over,
shortly? We must needs be brief,
seek to include everything.
        In our absence the house opens its books
and reads aloud to itself.
It is really evening, and everything stands out
individually, sacred-sobering and sacrosanct.

"The other side of the landscape," you say.
Would you like to go there? Is it a question of squeezing
        through, of reaching something?
We stop here. The landscape is too
inevitable to be on the map. We would like to
be able to contain it, but it keeps on turning
the most obvious side in our direction.
        The key: To keep on walking.
The guests lock themselves in the toilet
and use all the hot water.
But today it doesn't matter. We needn't
        care less. We give a friendly smile and do not
come to our senses again.

I let in the blind cat.
It has a mole in its mouth.
The mole also has five
fingers on each hand, a workman with
calluses from the underside of the landscape.
The guests fall from the trees
        and get concussion.
Evening comes and lies down nervously
around us: it has caused more lights to be lit

than it can manage to put out.
     Somewhere in the landscape it dreams
of falling stars and earthquakes.
Backwards through trains of thought, the things light up
like green diodes. Upwards from coffee at the bar
     the badly drawn map from the school biology book
suddenly remembered, where the body lay spread out
over the cerebral cortex: The big hands, the big lips,
     the tongue, the throat, the genitals, arms, eyes.
We are deformed cyclopes, stretching out
long-limbed towards an imaginary twin.
Keep going. Upwards in italics.
The landscape writes and writes.
     Now: Thoughts pumped out of the steps' rhythmic
snoring. And afterwards: How will it all turn out?
The money crumbles like old newspapers. Keep going.
There lies the house on the mountain in the landscape. Etc.
     A wide-open mouth in mid-agreement.
I walk straight in. My twin stands at the door,
     stretching out a gigantic hand.

For some reason I have come down to the seashore.
What am I doing here? Lindshipe?
     The guests say: The landscape is a sea.
But it is not so. It is: Nowhere.
A storm is
brewing. I leave the sea and the clouds as what
they are: Sketches of a landscape.
     The sea corrupts.
The swallows crowd together. We too
would like to be able to fly,
wouldn't we, Leonardo?
But the flying machines we invent keep falling down.
     I am not sure about this: An old coat.
Perhaps I've forgotten something of myself
absentmindedly? Something green from the landscape?

There's a man in front of the house in an old coat,
        chopping wood. It could have been me.

Shall we begin?
Clear announcement: The words blossom.
But the landscape is shy,
        it so easily sinks under the weight of all these pairs of eyes.
The guests phone and say thanks for a great evening.
We already miss their cheerful voices.
The trees at the top of the hill bear fruit.
        An arm reaches me an apple. There is actually
a hand at the end of the arm
and an apple in the hand, but the arm itself
is attached to nothing. The hand waves.
The doors open: The swallows fly southwards.
        The poem is a path through the landscape.
It turns and turns,
and it is that path I am to take.

Pia Juul

~

Denmark

Translated by Barbara Haveland

witch

we choose horses. I pick first and
Daddy gets the best. in the woods we shall
meet my beloved by the tree.

down the road the gallop pounds. I shall be a
fairy and a princess before the finish. but the stone
shines out to us. soon it will be
too late.

with all of my herbs at my belt.
doubled up. taut. my father feels
secure. he knows my drafts. thinks
I threw the hemlock away.
of that there is most.

when the black one bolts I
am ready. my hair comes loose. unseen
hands at work. the rein
cuts into my hand. wild winter.
see my breath so grand and glorious
in clouds. the snorts of the animals.

when they stop we have come through.
there Mommy sits and sews
my red bridal sheet.
wise Mommy. we wink.

*

not that it's of any use to you
of course. you're all in black. you
blend into her
darkened room.
you'll have to open doors onto light
yourself. the better to see
for yourself how everything is
on fire perhaps. or
not. she is indeed a
miracle moving there as
she does. the consummate
tension in her limbs is
an uncertain shot of
childhood memory which
she reuses and again and
yet again.
your toss of the head
determines her words.
surely you see that, miracle
maker

*

it's there to see in
the kaleidoscope, inherited
the forefather's glass hands
put together the cylinder
the mirrors and the colored
fragments

the Cyclopean sleep is
nothing to
the watchful eye he keeps
on all that she stirs
X-ray round the room
captures each raise of the head
she makes each step
she takes

∗

women's legs

dressed up. dressed down. young women
lying with one another
on the grass. bees humming. scythe cutting.
brook babbling. giggles.
they hide themselves. undressed.
run off in confusion. with
hair undone, with eyes
downcast. changelings, masquerading.
sashaying. richer. strong.

smack into the husband's
long look. his care
with his arm, a long arm.
so assured. with the ring on
her finger. belief in his wife.
her nape bowed and bare.
as the neighbor's. the grocer's.
the men's women. little
girls. unspeaking. bows. with
downy napes shining. the sun
in the sky. the coffee. the cognac.
the waist. skirts rustling.
legs hidden. but they are
there. the legs.

*

she deserves to be
killed for the pretexts she
uses the tricks she
plays with all the
looks she turns
inwards and up

her smoothness
her innocence redolent of
main meal in the middle of
the day that's French

a cloudburst has soaked her
to the skin

she has looked into
the sun

*

Tired out you lean
against the door and wait
the day is gray
the woods lean in towards the house
the clouds hang low over the roof
      He runs before you
The first step you take
is limp, is the vaguest
there could be, you are soft as
the color of the day
      He runs before you
it's simply a matter
of stretching out your leg
foot first, and you really
do try, how you try
      He runs before you

Novel

I let them wake up one morning in a big house with
almost empty rooms. Bedclothes don't rustle
because they are soft from use.
One of them is thin
The other is not naked - it is a woman,
she is dressed in lots of layers of fabric, there is silk and wool,
tulle that prickles, wool that itches, all of them black,
she won't take them off
she never takes them off, but he has touched her,
now he touches her again,
and she sighs, she is warm,
there are so many clothes
she says nothing, she touches back,
he is lying almost under her side,
he is nothing but skin,
that's how it should be, that's how it is, that's how it
has been all night long. I let them lie where they have woken,
they can go on lying there, let them lie, let that his clothes
have got lost, let the doors be locked, let them always
lie there, let her be warm, let it rub off on him, let
the rooms echo around their sounds, let them be.
Let them be

And oh for a watchman
down here on the street
to shatter that silence
with shouting and song.

Of all the sundry Torments
For myself I choose two:
The Snow and the malign Stench
Confidently I hold to the thought
that Life is long
I tell myself this in the night
Tell Navel
Tell Lips
Tell Eyebrows
and all gnaw their own Tongues
What an invigorating Punishment, to gnaw one's own tongue
I laugh at the thought of Lightning and Blood
But Snow and Stench would be torture to me
It is already here
Wet, cold, stinking everywhere
We think we are
all somehow connected
but there's nothing to this
Quite by chance
we stumble over an exquisite stone
and both bend down to it
at the same time
Oh - fate, I cry and clutch at my heart

*

The King of Castile
was in love with the Virgin Mary
And I too am
wild about a dream
The lighted windows the red ceiling
I saw from the dark
drove me mad
I howled like a dog
I whistled like a corner-boy
And people walked by
open-mouthed
as I stamped my way
across the square
I come walking along the side
of the wall
cautiously over the stones in the dark
almost blind
I come to follow that path
Summoned
I am challenged, who goes there?
And that I cannot tell

✻

We return to
the death
We cut the body down from the branch
We lean in horror against the rotten flesh
Fascinated we observe
the intimacy between
the detective and his chronicler
They have found
a long fair hair
on a lapel
Is it yours or mine
It is me who is dead
It is you who are rotting
We amuse ourselves in this grave
with worms in our mouths
and every eye peeled
our bones sticking out
through the skin
We discuss the plot and whine
it was you who did it
but that wasn't enough
If you're going to kill me
you must do it properly

*

nor did I want what I wanted
And what it was that I wanted I did not know
I did so want to have you
And lo and behold I got
what I wanted, and what do I do
I shout *what bliss* and
cry myself to sleep in broad daylight
They say one walks through
the meadow, and the meadow is not a
meadow, but something quite different
But can one pick
flowers where no flowers grow?
Yes. And then dive
straight in, bite
that bliss to bits, munching, gnawing
and gurgling, out of breath, sucking it
off and feeling sick. Stumbling
over the words, swallowing one's food,
blowing those three wishes all
too fast and all amiss. Witless and bewitched.

*

They wept when I
was conceived, they sobbed
and their sobs sounded
in the labyrinth of my non-existent
ear, and are resounding
there, still

I grew good at weeping

The weight
moves me
to weep, I mean
the burden of bones and hair
and the grinding of teeth in
my ears. And they tore
houses down, they tore the houses
down outside, and I was weighted
down, by bones by hair by the teeth
and all those words, where
do they come from all the words
and at this acclaimed hour
Put a lock on the door
Leave these houses be
Throw this through the air
Do not aim. You cannot
help but hit home

*

My Uncle Hector said
(though I've probably told you this before)
He was on his way down from the Hill
He had the sun in his eyes
then he said
as the children came running by
He said
no he said
The children came running
Then he said the same thing
as Knud once said
in another way
now I say it again myself
I can see him clearly
with the sun in his eyes
the lilacs on the Hill
this scent about Uncle Hector
And then he would always go
like so with his hand
Like so

*

"Oh no, my dear dancing master Rosenkilde,"
I said out of breath
- I cannot go on
Now we meet, now we part out on the floor
once too often have I
played about, been twirled about
under an arm, I'm feeling
too warm, now the room's
not just spinning, now I'm dizzy in the head
now I'm going to throw up
now I feel ill

I shall *never* ever be well
again, I'll probably be a poet
with a view of a church spire
and a man will cry:
Do *not* write
about it, never mention that spire
Yon dramatic Norwegian Løveid eyes
me and sighs:
Well I'd have said -
you should've killed him dead ...
Alright, I know, but
hark, is that someone clearing their throat:
How do you do. I am the one who awards
the Nobel Prize. Oh, it's such a hard job
awarding the Nobel Prize,
really quite exhausting. I have
just awarded it, so now I am
a bit tired. Forgive me.

It is not as if
I belong here
But who
would not
dance in the blue
with a whispered song in their ear
For the loft behind a stage
is barely to be seen

The room spins round
the upturned face
The room spins round anyone
who cannot see that loft

*

My Uncle Hector said (- said I -
with an assumed name, but the name is Holger)
My Uncle Holger said
(though I've probably told you this before)
He was on his way down from the Bank
He had the sun in his eyes
then he said
when the children came running by
He said
no he said
now Knud Erik says it
and his three sons do
and I do too
say the same thing, almost the same thing
We echo each other more or less
We buried the dog
on the Bank
and the dog was by turns called
Lassie and Jensen (Jensen was blind)
and Hugo and Hannibal
there on the Bank
my Uncle Holger
(because Holger was in fact his name)
Knud once said it
in another way
now I say it again myself:
Will you - or shall I?
I can see him clearly
with the sun in his eyes
the lilacs on the Hill
that scent about Uncle Hector
And then he would always go
like so with his hand
Like I told you before
- like so

NICOLAJ STOCHHOLM

~

DENMARK
TRANSLATED BY BARBARA HAVELAND

XII

I have spread myself over my face today
thought that person I cannot name
and am crushed through the 8th floor's crystal balcony
in a timeless fall that ends blindly
before that person I will not name
I have seen the sun today, it is all I can feel
I cannot bear it when it sinks
for the luminous dreams come with the darkness
extinguish my thoughts and leave me naked
so I must begin each and every day like you

EVENING FALCON

An evening falcon circles the fringe
of the verse crying all the while
                                gie gie gie
the forest the voice you have
carried up to this prospect:

                    Lifted above the ground the tower
                    is woken from the long sleep
                    on the snow in the shade a ring
                    of strong and burning souls
                    step into the center, New Year's morn

Ash tree, the willows' dark crowns
are thirsting hands raised aloft
a crystal garden that would seize
the blood like a railway line
half planted again in the ground

                    The fire burns, the trains grow
                    through the earth, through the tower
                    force that gives the mortal a
                    tongue, the untouched, the silent
                    the track I at last can leave behind

No heaven, no earth, no
height, no depth, no name
is it the beginning can it become
time or point back to the word
I in a deeper form

Hero outcast from the first
you were all names, united
you were the sea, the rock, the hope
sweetly conjoined and the page grew
into the air like the city

in early evening illuminated apartness
can I, transparent wrath
now call man's and woman's
one-sided obsession with mirrors
the crash in the collective memory

Seven men sleep with their faces
in the round stone, their wills
are rigid and stripped of perceptions
traveling in the night, they are the image
of the flesh chased across the sky

INJECTION

God is all faces, in the church
on the square, on the street, in
the store, in transit, on the door
in saying grace, on the needle
that blends blood with shadows
through your skin, at the cross-
road with red and white cars
rushing from fingertip
to fingertip, sebastian, see
bastian on his way with bull-
eyes like cells in the country
below, a cross turning slowly
around the moon, a hearing
in the names of god, orion
with stars under the skin
hits you blindly with
another sex the very first
day on your own, go to the
side, go to the right with your
lone chance, receive
the euphoria shot into
your busy center, a face
behind the curtain, on the mattress
where you lie naked now

(TRANSLATED BY THE POET WITH SUSANNE JORN)

SIOBHAN

Wheat houses in dawning blaze
a spark that springs from roof to
roof and treats the sky like
water, my heart taken
by the sea golden on its
bed of immolated coals in the room
now afire with
the longing to see you
return down the
fading moonway
outside the house where
the bushes are woken by a
troubled dream and the hill
rears up with a shadow
stabbed by the stars and a
white owl's headlong flight
take it from me, Siobhan
and set the sky on fire

SCYLLA & CHARYBDIS

Our Father, which art
so close, may our
begetter expire, may he be devoured by worms
in wounds that do not heal
the silent man, Mothers' Aid
your daughter is pregnant, January
crabs its way through the children's home
although the idiot screams from the sun
that it should bloody well be removed
brittle drops under
the tree and the grave turns
around, who are we
felon's daughter, queen
mother, all that water
through my lives, the door
that cannot be closed
closes now and we weep
violated, no more we weep,
we are become one again
and we take these outcasts

LOVEPUNKS

First your dark glance leading
me along your tremulous
marble skin and shooting me back
to my own life, then the waltz across
the table decked out with staggering
notions surrounding the time we but
read into the little mirror of sex,
you look and I know there and then
that we two are now going to weave our way
carelessly homeward among all the others who are
wending more gracefully on through
the night that of course belongs to everyone -
but this poem belongs to us! And you
smile right out to the finger tips of
my body as you turn the key in the
lock and I tear down your pants
and with a half-circle spread
your legs, my hand down there around your
cheeks wraps around your cunt and lifts you
rocking to the compass of the bed where
you are loosed from your restraints
and can glide, like the free part of the sea
rippling down over my cock
and show me the landscape departed
as it truly is, shatteringly
clear, breathtakingly black as your eyes
when my sperm cells hit your egg
and you dig your nails into my flesh

AMONG SIRENS

Someone or something is singing
three as with one mouth and
pointing exclusively at me:
a calcified X-ray leaf
a soul, repeat, a graft
of the tear that my father
fearlessly dropped and placed
my grandfather therein like
a boat of drunken love
women who have turned
into monuments and
have mistaken me for
a red light: yes, it is me
both sailing away from
and towards my own
swelling shadows and I
with the entire chorus
reply: that I am
no one and besides
I am on my way home

DAYTRIP

My heart is in heaven, my heart
full as it is of air and smoke

The ties of memory are loose, tongues
weaving covertly, naked and babbling
stone circle in the fields, the white
shell a pierced shadow in the dark
a blind spot the eye turns around
I see grains graved with the word I
cannot comprehend, a bird flurries up
great clouds on the slide of ash leaves
and behind me the night lies unfolded
to a sky in which all the stars would
be writ in capitals for I have lost
my place and stand now cloaked by sight
staggering towards the side I would leave
blank to the gathering after the sleep
church, meadows lying under the pallid
vault of winter's drift over amputated leaves
a glance's curving cups for windswept water
no one's script can inhabit without being
joined to an earthen, breathless
kinship from the waves to the well
where the image is shot to rest a moment
through the surface with sight failing and
the maid of dread, the dam of absence stands
clear in each fire pond, each nest of creatures
among the blind I have sent flying
like a tent pulled up by the force without a
move from me towards the still point
in the bed or on the table let's call it
a center running away from itself or
locked up inside a beating room with the air
up and down the stairs to a door, a sheet
pulled over the head, reflection, a meeting
embracing of own blood by a hundred
expired roses to leave a trace, a bullet

planted before the beginning's word is heard
like no one's cry back to the long drought
seen through the rain, from the bonfire ground
the sound sails quite cut off through open
throats under the ships of stone in the fields
a redbreast flies up, stamens of coal
turn to ashes, turn to dust, the dust raises
a town outside the town with red walls around
action around space, etched in the hand
and from the branches the voiceless women sing
from the east in you wind
to the west it is blind
and I who come with a line, a speech
I come from my fireside, I am come
like a dancing flame of my own house
the white ash tree outside takes the moon's
place, I walk towards a circular building
flaming progress through all the ages of the tree
stained furniture, a charred navel that
coils its way up to a figured glass dome
spider eyes splintered by the sun, staring out
until I am a ledge in the wind folded in
like the wave dragged from a hook, a knot
stiffened in its form   unborn in its form
        stilled in its form
I am here ((the Mallarméan violin
I suspend the ash in the air, I draw
breath elsewhere) twice I built
my house where nobody threw me out
(where no one will find a place, where nothing
took place)) I am found behind the whore
and the traffic's bright eyes on the way to all things
stamped out on the spot, the round oven
at the base of the tower under the red glass
where the high chess players congregate
with horny hands tossing the bishops away
across the table in the sand to the foot of the

one, the shaman in the chamber's midst who holds
the eye captive while round himself he turns
to the left, you cannot do it
right about, why do you do it
with the malformed boy under the blanket
like a spirit stone in the corner that merely
draws my sight back, chess players like firewood
in the salt air, the telegraph's white tongue
the radio plays music, a song over fast
over heard, taken by itself, the song
kneads the bread is not our food sings
the ghost of the song, the water not a fluid
do not drink the water from their river, do not eat
the seed from their fields where the self grows
sleepless rosy-lipped severed eyelids
my infinite devices blend in with
my guise, children drink from my breast my
mighty nipples embrace all parables, steep
as ladders before the milk burns through
their years, by a fire at the center or on a
beach in the storm with no other light
in the spaces between
Our words to the mass, the square root
artificial flowers forever fair in hothouses
of CO_2, semen, secretions, sum of feathers
lost and signs lifted like bounding shields
acres of swords in forests of glue under
the ash's unfurled beacon, divided root
fastens around the stone carved into a heart
with the one hand, a fiery axe
another nails the power of the fire to my word
and deliriously encodes it through veins as
the hothouses' disconnected light, the forsaken
spiral of shadow I shall wholly drive out
captivating negatives of my own form
nigh on feminine in its reference, almost
prosaic in the way the urge to break

coils up between my breasts and
works them deep into my body until
they reach our wills, my eyes that are
almost staring back at the darkness
from which I with my body can shape the world
we see me, mid the radiance in our circle
we see me, the only change in our
path which I decoratively tread out with
irresistible hips succulent with mint
the strongest that can never be
an image and we receive me with the
tenderness granted to us, the shadows our lot
my anger's naked trees, the only black
line in a snow-covered landscape, the only
dark mast among all the white, the height
over its own constructions in the snow, our lot
our tracks pregnant as the butterflies'
imprint on the wind, as the wind's unheard mark
upon the sea, as the scales of the wind recorded in an
observatory where the planets course down
the wall like vowels through a body
between leaves
a landscape almost possessed by wanton
productivity, appointed by cathedrals
which with blessings each thistle tongue
calls after voices of stone, minimal
subjects mustered on deck, outside
the sea clear between houses washed clean
of all states, mirrors in shops
boats in the harbor, little black box constructed
with entrances masculine, feminine
from this I fly and see them drown
prows turned up to the sun a moment
that lets the flame speak out across the sea
till the mirror is swept clean and ring free
behind me the town is bathed in gloaming
you are here, blown in from every corner

the light from the lamps opens you
and again I am of and in your eyes
your words reach the sound on my lips
send steps rebounding through
outer chambers, dividing up passages like roses
with my personal equation in water in fire

The Mirror Invites

You machine, the skylark lives, a heart
out in space, I can feel it beating
in the same way as mine, it's the sound of
flies and paper talking in tongues
at night when the shadows cross
before my eyes and tether themselves
like blind horses, tonight we shall break
you and I, through the ocean's warm
meshes sticky as newborn babes
dream our way up to heaven's scorched
hornblowers where we can rest a while
and let the animals graze, see
our shadows touch the earth it
holds us as we climb
all the way to the stables of the stars:
a man sits watching
the deep blue of morning near sinking
down into the dark mold, we know
the riddle of procreation splintered
like a ball of fire, we have seen
the captain spin on his own axis, we
have received the call from the dead
telephone, we have waited in vain for
all the other weatherbeaten souls in the capital
of the wind, he is gone, the life
we left behind we have no
need of here where we radiate
the same purpose, we can see through
each other's long prisms of shattered
remembrance, let their shining new
signals discover the body in the
holy mind
                    do you hear

LARS SKINNEBACH

~

DENMARK
TRANSLATED BY BARBARA HAVELAND

I DON'T CARE who you are
I don't care about your kindnesses
I don't care what you do
I don't care what you've done for me
I don't care about what you could do
I don't care that you'd like to be my friend
Piss off, you jerk or I'll cut off your legs
Piss off, you jerk or I'll cut off your legs

It's a terrible thing when you finally find yourself
and can't find your way back

like in the glove that somebody must have dropped
in the driveway, to lie there
pointing in all directions

I see my parents in the rain and the garden
and the fence
like in a jigsaw puzzle from days gone by

What's new pussycat? There's no relief
in the weather, in the everyday

I see a shirt in the drying loft
sleeves hanging down to the floor
as if the body had got lost during a yoga exercise

Somebody must have dropped the town from a great height
scattered like the shards of a cheap vase

What's new pussycat? There's no relief

BIRDS MIGRATING draw
draw a world in their wake
on strings from their feet, it's evening
somewhere, maybe there's a war
in the eyes of a man
taking his rest
under a sky shot down

It's raining
The tin roof's singing
Darkness falls
through fine-meshed curtains
The trees outside
are drawn all in black
Maybe it's night
as the world breaks loose of sight

Somewhere you can hear the sea
drawing the years in its wake
and the distances
and sorrow
Sometimes you have to sink down into it
or else pretend it isn't there

There's a smell of barbecuing, the killing of the family
is celebrated, deep among
lilac bushes and old hate

I love Denmark, occupied as it is by ghosts
with painted human forms
and crows that sing Carl Nielsen

And the meat turns in the throat, the last
before the darkness is carried out in porcelain cups
with fragile little ears

that listen to a young girl's song
She has decked herself in plumage and regurgitates her food
after every meal

IT'S MORNING and we seem almost ourselves
The pigeons sit and shit on the window-sill
I push up the window and picture my hands
fluttering off into the sky, they would so like
to build a palace for wet dreams. It's too early
for a shag you say and tip over the milk carton
We're happy really, but we ought to talk a bit less
be more edifying
The bread and honey bears the imprint of my teeth
The coffee steams up into my face, it would so like
to be a dark cloud. It's too early to miss you
I think to myself and think of that missing
that is as sharp and irritating as a broken tooth
you simply can't help
poking with your tongue

TIRSTRUP

We had bought some plaice and walked about
as if the days were pulling themselves to their feet

At the dinner table the sentences seemed
to fondle a confined rapture

For the fourth day in a row we were on the beach
the wild roses
reminded me of something

In the evening the trees seemed to draw closer to the house
as if wishing to book into the least of edens

In the end we woke one morning
and took a picture that developed itself

The least I can do is to hold it close
when even the least is enough

MY GIRLFRIEND SINGS IN THE KITCHEN, she has given me
a grasshopper in a cola bottle
it chews on stalks and gazes with wonder
at the constellation in my eye. So
I became a grasshopper god, I think
and put the bottle down

My girlfriend has no family, she sings
from the bottom of her loneliness
and lies in the garden in the summer
while I stand with my eyes turned to the sky
and think that everything is good

There are times when we love each other so much
that somebody has to drive us out
of their thoughts

There are so many questions and so little we have to do
People are killing one another in Denmark, can you see a way out?
We lay in your bed and licked one another clean of feelings
The town and the autumn blow the brain away, it can sound so sweet
in your ears, through holes in the skull and the houses
do they come crashing down in delight? The trees play a solution
in the wind, while an old man pees in his pants
Those were the days. There are so many days
And prophecies. When the dog barks
in your neighbor's house, the king suffers
from chlamydia. We can make victims of ourselves
is that modernism's way out, the debased individual?
Symphonic trees with skeletal fingers
knock discreetly on the window. There is no conductor
to gather the world on the tip of his baton
or to explain it in sign language for anesthetized eyes
Do the houses collapse like a dead man's lungs?
Is love replaceable?

FAIRY TALE

He carried me home, alive. Tomorrow will be there tomorrow again
a quiet wind perhaps, contents, you sit in the courtyard

with white triangles on your breasts, your bikini hanging to dry
like a truth in the breeze, it is afternoon, yes it is

or else it is morning and the weather is fine, actually I think
I love you. We walk along the street in thin shirts

and we're drunk, the breeze, don't forget the breeze and the
     clouds setting shoulders to the wheel
till they look like identities and the rain under lampposts

like horses' heads snorting, can one make a wish when they snort?
there's so much rain, it speaks for itself, that's how

it sounds, listen, the radio in the morning, weather forecasts
     and the courtrooms
acquitting a suicide, fresh snow, my ears scrunch, the dark

has just woken, the mind constantly drifting over the land
casting shadows, can one punish the dead? I wish

that we may always be together, the warmth of summer, the
     lakes and the sea
your back bending forward in bed, what do you wish for

you would ask, your sex and the wind tugging at the doors, at our faces
the dead who come to visit us at night, by day, we play

games and laugh and the slender trees in the parks shield us
from the world and the cars that drive in and out of the world

and you see that the clouds are gathering, does that mean something?
Clear skies and the lies we are so fond of, other

things we love, the stars are so far away now, everybody knows that
and we throw the dice in matrimony

and say you win, I don't care and I open the window
or put my ear to your navel, there are shells

that speak of oil slicks and shipwrecks, I'm randy as a sailor
Look, the rubbish men's footprints in the courtyard, when the
　　frost comes down

suddenly one morning they formed a face, a posh mug
but by the time you got up again, too late. The coffee

that condenses, coffee in the afternoon in a garden in the sun
is it going to rain, one might ask, is it clouding over?

And the cars on the outskirts of town, mimicking the sounds of the wind
the slip-roads, resembling the contours of an enormous ear

like fossils they lie there listening, I miss
your breasts, the sun's pattern in them, the rain and the predictions

to be drawn from the weather, deluges, domestic flights
People fly kites and we lie and kiss, it's cold

vacationing in the underworld, oh, your stomach rumbles and later
in the winter the beach rolls out

like a white carpet and the Queen of the Sea sits in audience,
　　that's how it goes
can one make a wish? I would so like to wish

that we may always be together, something constant
in the gloaming, the early evening, with the smell

of cooking, you wine and dine your parlor ghosts
I love you, it's gonna rain, it's gonna rain

+

It's essential to wash oneself, to cleanse oneself, we're waiting
for a ferry, the cars look so patriotic in the long lines

What do you do? Pack cars, if someone shoots someone in a wood
you read about it in the paper, the exception becomes the rule,
     people shoot

one another in Denmark, I'm a bit tired, you say, someone else
says he's going to sell his trailer and sells his trailer

and before too long it's rusted up, it's sacred, and I love
all the green and all the yellow and there's no one

who is my friend, there's no one who is my friend or rather
there's no one and then suddenly: there's my friend and you
     are pregnant

or you've given birth to a girl, Caesarean section, cut out of the belly
that's the stuff of myth, and before that my father died and
     before that. We drove

along high roads and trunk roads, ring roads and country roads,
city roads and dirt roads and we took the ferry across

and played cards and I won or Dad won, at any rate
Mom lost and that was that

and when that that was that we had to muddle through yet another grief
and when that was that we had to bring up our own children

and when they were those who grew up, we had to kick them out
of the houses, of the societies, out of our lives

or put them back to bed, carry them back home, hungry, stupefied
dead of broken hearts, drowned in soft values

The old folk weep and wail, they are the victims of so much.
　　Only the dead
can cross the highways unscathed, i.e. remain in the same state

in which they started out. My legs are too short to reach the ground

YOU HAVE TO BE WILLING TO FAIL. Thanks for the invitation
At night when we lie sleepless, we pour our lives into bottles
and then we fall over, it's awfully hot in here don't you think?
He has a suitcase full of public bills and run-down virtues
These are the means of our revolutionary hero. And the end?
Generosity, perhaps. There must be more important things to discuss
than public information, Oh, d'you think so? The sun skulks
between the houses, people languish in age-old darkness. One says
Then another says. But it's a migration
and as such will engulf and drown the western world
if we don't - well, if we don't watch out
This is the privileged defending their privileges!
This is the privileged defending their privileges!
There are so many predictions. And pigs. If you piss
in the Muslim Sea it'll only grow bigger and smellier
But don't let that stop you, Mr. Member of Parliament, sir
A little dignity, on the other hand. Will it rise? Will it rise
to a clean-up? One or another ought to hang themselves in a wood
so dense that no one will be burdened with finding the body
That is humanism. Do you regard it more as a death threat?
You can if you like. They lack the will to get out of their beds
they lack the courage for almost all feelings

I DON'T BELIEVE IN FRAGMENTS, they plummet off
the bridge over the Great Belt, through accident, by accident
personify them or turn them into suicides
in a dense wood. Knowing yourself is cheap
between island and island. Have you conscience enough
for a whole life? Men are more numerous than lice
Page 22. Have you a plan? Something to do with infinity
The highways look like rivers that only the dead can cross
Is it mortal dread that moves us to pass laws
which cause our lives to imitate life
in the strictest kingdoms of the dead? The lawgivers, the rulemakers
and the value-setters, let them administrate a fun fair
for the dying. But that's just what they're doing. There has to
be a day and a better way to Tirstrup. Page 23
Always remember how far you've got and leave no marker
I may do it all, I may be everything
Pissing scares off the evil spirits
Wearing a pale-blue shirt

A FISH IS SLICED open in the kitchen, he knows its entrails
they promise the fall of the state and great good fortune
There is too much ill fortune in the house and the winter, the cold
does it make the walls seem more intimate?
They show so much on the TV, why do we love
the lie? I can't live without you, you know, those trumpets
Ah, but winter came anyway, unreal and I promised
always to maintain the depth in my strayings
Remember your safety instructions. You might be able
to save a ferry from going down. Ivory moon
The night is sensitive fingertips, adroitly they play
upon your self-perception. Why not take up the welfare state?
Instead of finding depths in ... A bit of a squeeze? Can you keep time
with the highest political goals. Go on, turn the people
into an orchestra, any one will do. No responsible person
can regard a low life expectancy or lack of education
as positive values, they say. Might one also say
Regiment the people! He lies and waits, the lung patient,
for yet another feeling to go down. The question is
when. You call your dogs to you. I reply
Mankind is ugly

To FOLLOW OUR INSTINCTS in the old colonies. Later we had drinks
on the deck and the night was an unknown narcotic. Want to come?
You should have been there. Then we went home. Mankind
is a growth that's only just begun to see that it's a disease.
Think about it. Again? No, come on, think about it
Thanks for the arrogant service. After that what is there to say?
That my mind is playful today. And that to follow our instincts
our natural inclinations will be our downfall
Slacken all sails. The night sky experienced by a blind man
It happened too fast. One must remain polite to one's nearest
and dearest to the last, right to the last. How long do you have?
I don't believe that any person, mystic or enlightened dog
experiences the world as greater than I do:
already it pervades everything
Nostalgia is a degradation of feeling
Every outburst of feeling is a degradation of feeling
You don't want to look a fool forever

THAT IS WHY THEY REVILE YOU
That is why they ignore you
That is why they ridicule you
That is why they piss on you
That is why they hate the sight of you
That is why they despise you
That is why they won't listen to you
That is why they don't give a shit about you
That is why they belittle you
That is why they are sick to the stomach of you

DIDDA

~

ICELAND
TRANSLATED BY THE POET WITH BERNARD SCUDDER
& GORDON WHALMSLEY

PASSION

I am never above suspicion.
I am the centrifugal force of the unexpected.
I am the passion daughter of waking and dreaming.
I am Little Red Riding Hood entering the forest again and again.
Sleeping Beauty slumbering away century after century, dreaming
never wishing to awaken.
I am reality and existence and my sisters sorrow and joy.
They sing with me when we feel the urge.
I am electricity in light and in the electric chair as well.
I am unspoken yet yelling bloody murder.
I am faith in hope and hope in faith.
I am prosaic yet rhyming all things.
Rich in nothing, full of everything,
I empty and I fill.
I am my own opposition,
daring all and hiding everywhere.
I am good when I am bad and worse when I am at my best.
Life in life and death in death.
I am written and I am told,
played and read,
painted and explained.
I am requested when everyone will have more.
My father loves me and even dares to say so out loud.
My mother finds me within her and on her and she believes in me.
I am a perfect child, a bastard,
a love child, unintentional.
I am an accident.

I am organized chaos.
I am long desired.
I am all of a sudden.
I am the liberator of the mind from the heart.
I am flaming water and soaking fire.
I am what you are and what you do not wish to be.
I am consonance with dissonance.
I speak when silence is demanded.
I am silent when answers are required.
I am bent and also straight.
I am the knife in the wound,
the core of things.
I am the tear in the heart and the leitmotif of the limbs.
I am the body inside and out.
I am all he desires but cannot understand in words.
I am the sucking drain of day and the breezing fair wind of night.
I am with you when you leave and with you when you come.
I am open at both ends but close up as soon as everything
    goes out of me.
I have never died and have never been born.
I believe in you yet you always lose.
I am the only one who can hear you think, forcing you
to tell even against your will.
I am the spirit in the blood, the spirit in the wine.
I am a poison storing up and consuming.
I am the bite in the knife.
The cry from the wound.
The umbilical cord.
The last straw.
The most obvious and least visible to you alone.
I am passion.
True love of all dreams.
The power in all streams.
I am and have to be, so that
all that is may become nothing.
So that nothing may become something all by itself.

TODAY

No, today I don't plan
to be melodramatic
and compare my self with a dried
rose hanging upside down on a string.
No, I shall compare
myself with the figurehead on
a pirate ship, plowing
through it all with
bare salty breasts.

MOTHERLAND

Under the heavens
lies a fossilized
mountain-woman*
of a dwarf state
with the huge drill
of our father
thrust inside her.

*mountain-woman is Iceland's national icon of independence.

OUT

You're so far from "in"
that even the
automatic doors
don't notice you
and you can't be seen
in the shopping mall mirrors
and people don't say "sorry"
when they walk all over you.
And if nothing happens
that can drive you
through it all
then you'll just become
a flabby spear
on the end of a thread.

EAT ME

Eat me alive
eat me blistering
with horniness
eat me ice-cold
with hot sauce
eat me lukewarm
and purple
eat me all
inside
eat me all
outside
but never again
pour vodka
into my navel.

TOWER

There's something so incredibly powerful about bulls' tongues.
They're so strong, big and grabbing.
I once knew a bull called Tower and his head was so big I could
have camped out inside it.
He hated me and cursed me every time he saw me and it was
important always to keep a head's length away from him,
otherwise he banged his head against your thighs and sent you
flying along the fodder range.
But I forgot to consider his tongue.
So once when I was mucking out from the cows I turned my
back at him.
And as I stood straight in front of him I felt something thick,
like a gigantic man's palm, slip between my thighs and press up
tight against my crotch. The pressure was so great that when
he pulled me towards him I had to let go of the broom and
clutch at another cow's stall. His tongue tugged at my pants
and I could feel the front of my panties rolling down.
His wet chops pushed up against my buttocks and his rough
snorting blew through my pants. In the fraction of a second
I had to react to what was happening, I simply came. And it
was a weird sensation to tear myself away from the grip of his
tongue, because really I would have liked more.
But he hated me, would have killed me if he had got hold of
me, and his ridiculous expression told me that he didn't have
the faintest idea what he had done to me.

NO ONE

It would be awful
if someone confused
themselves with me.
That's why I make sure
that I'm exceptional.
No one has this sort of
ear.
No one, precisely no one
has this sort of scar
on the inner thigh
of the left leg
from a wire fence
in London
the day the hurricane
passed over and I
and the bloke I met at the Dolphin
(whose name I never knew)
broke into his uncle's
caravan to have
a quick shag
while the little angry
dog lay growling
under the table.
No one.

Iceland's Honor

Me on board a trawler.
From Greenland.
Completely lushed
from spirits and beer.
My arms and legs just about holding on,
one side-turn from crashing out.
The Faroese was always trying to tell
the Greenlanders I was a nice person.
They just laughed and pinched me.
there were at least two I bunked with
but they were Danes.
So the Greenlanders went on
marking me with bruises and thumped
heartily on my shoulders.
And there I sat with them,
sang a song and there was whispering
of "jeg elsker dig" by many different voices.
And I felt like a fish factory girl
gutting away, up to my crotch in roe.
Tried to gather up the inferiority complex
of us small nations into one, but the only
thing I felt was this active empathy
and fathomless interest in the effects of firewater.
They'd started working up on deck,
so I put myself ashore with three
stolen beer bottles in my coat pocket,
and the lads at the landing bay laughed
and said something, and I told them
to shut the fuck up.
Me a trawler whore? NO!
I the sword of Iceland, its honor and shield, staggering
off into Tryggvagata Street.

Jeg elsker dig *is Danish for I love you. Iceland, Greenland, and the*
Faroe Islands once were all under Danish Crown, and we still have
to communicate amongst ourselves in the language of our former
oppressors. —D.

SIGURBJÖRG THRASTARDÓTTIR

~

ICELAND
TRANSLATED BY BERNARD SCUDDER

A VERY PLATONIC SIGHTSEEING TOUR

Didn't look too impressive
those ruins
yet they charged admission
and we waltzed around a bit
half-rushing because
there was supposed to be such
an amazing sunset
in a completely different part of the city
— our guide said
let's get a move on!
but I thought it was a shame
was half-hoping to bump into Plato
in the water-filled foundations
ask him better about that
love stuff
whether he'd really
never done it
but he wasn't quite there
that day
maybe he also thought they were
crummy ruins
p.s.
the sunset sucked

REYKJAVÍK II

I intend
to build you

sturdy silence
from washed-up pillars
that will withstand
the chill north wind
and heckling

a deep silence
from timber formwork
if the engines whir louder

solid silence
from senile oak
if nothing better turns up.

EUROPE

The airline will be offering a newfangled service in the future: boeing 737
jets are driven along highways on the continent of europe between
famous historic sites wine is served generously and the most popular
route is düsseldorf-naples because then there's time for three bottles of
beaujolais nouveau two crates of stella export and four glasses of asti
gancia at the minimum to drink toasts with randy wheat farmers
valiant tax evaders short-sighted prostitutes and other citizens of the
community who wave eagerly to the passengers when the jets roll past
with all their lights on for landing.

May I Hug You Again?

— green —

the following phenomena
fortify
when you leave:

cough mixture
the six o'clock weather
the laurel leaves you forgot
and the picture of Mr. Cave

— red —

I shouldn't be so close, you say
it's all so inflammable
but I'm here to water you, I say

— yellow —

the sun lights up
the top steps first of all
and Mr. Cave strikes the right note:

I'm exhausted by your absence

— blue —

I'm also
afraid of forgetting you
beyond that fishless sea
as you call it

but if I can tug
on your beard just one more time

then maybe

BEING FERTILIZED

Inside me
swims a fish
darting in circles and tickling
strange
feeling something alive inside you

doubtless it's a farmed fish
I've tried eating fish meal
to keep it happy
but still feel my innards being eaten
one after another

I know neither
how far I'm gone
nor what this is called
by others
maybe wishful thinking, fear,
orgasm

ALONE ON A GREEK ISLAND, I

Greece is black-and-white
I saw that
in the film about Zorba
it rains too
with such force
that the ferries are delayed
until ten o'clock

yet it isn't true
as is often claimed
that beautiful people
die there
to the riotous applause
of the ugly

in fact that often happens
but never here

AND YOUR TEARS

The bed stands
in the middle of the floor
the sheet sweeping cold tiles
I know you're thinking of here
day and night
that's why I'm lying still as the grave
beneath the white ceiling
which soon will blossom
for you are dying from me
night and day
I promised to lie
in the middle of the island
in the deepest valley
dearestdarling
and your tears glide down on parachutes of tulips
onto my quilt
that I may sleep

Home Delivery

A man comes cycling
into my living room
big-eared and dripping
riot oil
big-nosed and ripped pant legs
dismounts from his bike
big-mouthed but doesn't say a word
an oil slick on the floor
maybe I've stopped understanding people but
what does this man want
I consider offering him apple juice
then he ruins the silence
squint-eyed looks around and says:
yes, did you order a revolution?

ICE AGE

The snow never melts
in the ears of trolls
that have turned to stone
at dawn on the moors

rivers flow
dandelion slopes grow
but old ice glows
in rock-ears
for ages

and blessed are the trolls
for they know not
what they are missing

have never heard of
hardcore bands
air cushions
electric can openers

Action Squad: Operation 0402

I could have myself nailed
underneath the lounge table
face down
ankles and wrists in all the corners
I could have a glass with a straw
on the floor
maybe chocolate milk in the glass
there'd have to be a cloth
over the table and me
I'd have to take care not to sneeze
preferably in skin-tight clothes
breathe slowly show
patience >>> all that fuss
just to hear
how you talk
about me and the others
with your mouths full
of cookies
and the glasses from iittala
and georg jensen
in the glass cupboards
I shall leak
everything

STANDARD FEAR

I envy those who have memories
of war they have an advantage when it
comes to gratitude I feel peculiar
on new year's eve too many unexpected
bangs yet I could surely get by on
canned food like anyone else and
I'm also determined to keep a diary
like anna frank but until then I sleep in
and delay and varnish cabinets but sometimes
I most want to watch a cartoon
preferably a simple one for little children
since I don't know when maybe
the moomins but I was always scared
of the groke and I know she's here

ARABIA

Woman, get dressed
this instant
here is neither the place
nor the time for flesh
you're lucky to be able to go unseen

wear
preferably black
how lucky you are
if someone dies
not having to go home and change

get dressed
this instant
because your flesh is word
and here is only time for silence.

JYRKI KIISKINEN

~

FINLAND
TRANSLATED BY ANSELM HOLLO

FROM KUN ELÄN (AS I LIVE)

I

There was no need to die,
had to stay here
and remember too much,

remember the snowy path
the shimmering foliage and mud,
look at the red trace

on the pole flashing by
and leave a message
on the answering service.

II

It is easy to leave
without looking back,
without remembering

a child's words,
without enduring
the death of others,

without crawling out from
the scrap metal that was meant

to be a grave, to refrain

from waving when
the coffin continues
on its way, empty,

toward the permanent
exhibition of twisted
metal, toward

a child's strings of words.
So much time
in the warehouse,

no one lives there,
the lights are still on
in the cabs of trucks

but the door does not
open, we have so
little room

to live so long
it goes on when
you cast the die.

III

What did I think about
independence,
  he asked
by the roadside
and still
keeps asking, even though
it was all cleaned up right away

it took only a moment
for the page to heal
  a jungle
of words to shoot up, and it
  covered, covered

in that sense
sentences are conceived
  he pushes
    mike
      into mouth,   sense-
lessly,   in the ruins of

      freedom,   in the camp
        where the same man
still lives,

      he walks
the same
        alleys
    as
before,   buys
    the same
              foodstuffs,   in a moment's
madness   its capricious
        glitter   the road
leads to   the culprits'
        party   to a garden
where   we
    are compelled   to live
              this
accursed   day

                which
                is   a gift

    which
is   a gift

V

A man takes his hat from the doorman,
finds his car keys,

this is the warrior's fate: the desire
for power, over oneself at least,

to forget for a moment, grab the steering wheel,
defend his own lands, dreams, accounts:

to drive through the stone, determine
slavery's boundaries; shift up,

accelerate the expanse,
let the landscape flow unimpeded,

the view melts, dims
beyond dashboard and windshield.

He does what he wants, joins,
pierces, is born, dies, feels

himself to be real, just a light
pressure on the pedal and the stone's weight

disappears, just a small evasive motion
and the girder's hardness can't be felt,

anywhere. The coma of substance is over,
objects rise out of their graves,

the depths of their names, no need to
trudge anymore, the forest a dim

green line, no need for a coat,
the car is another climate.

No need for bodily strength,
just turn that key,

the window green as you like it,
your mind nothing but this lane.

VII

We are all
one coal,
a blind gambler's
stake
long ago.

the same old
hand still
works, it deals
the cards, the rocks
that fit in the hand,

so is it he who arranges
the stars in the sky,
the blind heroes,
the dead and the living,
the animals in the woods,

the eyes in the dark,
birds and machines
to fly in formations
spelling out
fate. your own.

hand must be
played without cheating
but with some
cunning, you must
make the most

of your cards,
the impossible.
My mind grows
the same rootstock
as this forest,

thought circles
the same track
as the planets
that travel
around

the sun's
invisible axle,
I turn away
but you always follow
hard on my heels.

VIII

Gravity knows
no mercy,

love always
attracts the one

who flees his
fingerprints

even though his hand
left them there as a sign,

wiped them off,
he flees

toward fast
deeds to realize

desire, when
the sun's mass

demands
everything, me,

you, the passion
that flees

behind your back,
behind my back,

as I am still alive,
and read the day,

it radiates off the page,
I write it.

X

Here is the well
where they found the skull
in which was born
the image of that god

who created the impala
that ran so fast,
that evoked envy,
that gives strength,

that causes deeds,
that gives birth to freedom,
out of which the human
builds its own image,

that tunes the machine,
that accelerates the car,

that gives birth to the god
who smashes the skull,

which is thrown in the well
that fills up with water
through which flows a current
to guide the spirit

that dreams the forest
that hides the well,
that pierces
the soul of a man,

in which a tree grows
a branch for a bird
whose song wakes the mother
who does not fly away.

XII

When you have seen your child dead,
      you are completely free,
the mother said,
      but she was wrong.
Scissors cut the umbilical cord,
break the mother's trap strings,
            but the child can't escape.
     An invisible hand,
invisible ropes still animate
              four limbs.
And the puppet does not collapse but
returns to leave,
         under a great shadow
free mushrooms,
     free children germinate,
mycelia spread across the boulder.

No one admits to a common debt,
      that goes without saying,
even though the rain never collects it.
The crow carries the seed, the seed carries the myth,
the legend, the knowledge recorded in plants.
The plant feeds the animals,
                         it grows leaves
below the window. The plants' story
surrounds him. He reads it.
Owes a debt to it. Does not admit that.

The stevedore secures the cargo, joins two
countries, continents:
      the hoe and the fork, they don't know
how to hate one another or how to admit
their common debt, the debt that
joins them.
As the diesel engine roars past, a flash
of silver gets out of the way,
          but the beast never says thank you, does not know
that it lives in the shade of one even
greater, eats its food.

When your own child is honored, you are complete,
                said the father
who did not know that he would survive his son.
The same vein still feeds them, because the family is one animal
                and the village one brain stem
whose thought a human being is, just as arbitrary,
                just as quick
as a lane change, a traffic pulse
before the morning rush hour.

XVI

Behind the broken windshield
objects tear themselves away from their names,

and you don't know even after returning home
to what use you should put, today, the lighter,

the coins or the car wax. But there
you sit, in your bony cave

and gaze at what flows before you.
You can't complain anymore. You don't complain.

XVII

On the table you find a knife and
fruit peels, a little
dried juice on the table cloth,

you open the balcony door to the street,
where you see not the century but
a petrified drop, a freeze frame

of your mind. You air out books,
pages, mind, wander endlessly
in a dream, almost reach the square.

The sun already killed the horse,
the old man and the flower seller,
what remains is white stone, a square

of virgin birth, so catch
the flash of death, soon even it
will be gone, an echo roams the ruins.

How suddenly the flock dispersed,
this square was born in the mind, in vain
you shout, look for her, outside

wandering figures you don't recognize,
are you talking to the dead, are you
dead yourself. Thought looks for another,

another that is a prisoner of itself,
its form. Break it, smash my shell
that looked for the form of a pearl, the grain

rubbed against the mucous membrane,
the muscle, the cavity, looked for
a dune. It did not get past the teeth, ever.

XVIII

He saw faces behind the glass,
heard himself breathe.

With his fingertips, he brushed the glass surface
but it was not the same as skin.

Slowly, he arranged what he saw,
that blurry motion, but it did not work

as an architecture, the kind
a living city is perennially building.

He opened up to a gaze, froze,
lost the game altogether.

Then the scythe disappeared. He opened
a window onto the street, heard

leaves rustle as if waking up
to life, one more time.

INTERMISSION

But I did not sing,
I chased her away,

flushed the toilet, paced
circles in the living room

like a moth that looks for
a place to land

or a solution that does not exist
to a problem that probably

does not exist either,
just a wall full of

leather-backed books
and seats among which

the moth chooses one, a
commodified insomnia

a landscape someone
invented once: palaces,

persons, tensions,
systems and maps

constructed by language insects
on top of the void,

in the air, an imago mundi
never seen before

never before heard of
utopias, illnesses

people prefer to endure
rather than

giving up, once they have
forgotten the war's causes

or the cornerstone of their learning
ground up to gravel

long ago, they still love
the country they have

destroyed, for love
is stronger than

its object, and who
needs it, the group

eats reason and everything learned,
it turns us into beasts,

the congregation executes
its christ, the state

its sages, but the sleepless
animal keeps wrestling

in the mud with its inner
hero, the beast; yearns, spits,

rages and grieves, looks for
reconciliation, tries

to mediate and interpret
between invisible enemies

to whom only sleep and murmur
can lend a shape, until the image

finally shatters
into sentences, steps

into line between covers,
on the shelf: in the closed pages

simmers yet another delirium
no one has ever seen before.

Helena Sinervo

~

FINLAND
TRANSLATED BY ANSELM HOLLO

TIRESIAS' PLEASURE

Few forget the sea
for one droplet,
but I don't remember
your face, only the drop
that hung from the tip of your nose
and fell into the wine glass.

Was I looking at you
or at myself, or at something
in between, I don't remember
but the incandescent light
struck that droplet and shimmered
and, shimmering, fell.

The wine still trembles.

THE RIDER

From behind the sun, out of the fiery lap of a particle storm
he landed below this reading lamp
and immediately charged from one room to the next,
        pennants streaming from shoulder blades,
and on the cloak, the early germs of identity,
        small enough to fit in a teaspoon.

Meadow and speedwells under his eyelids, what did he set out
to do?

To build a race track, then to kneel down
                on frail grass knees
                in front of his toys.

VISITING HOUR

Leave the door open, be so kind.
Nothing compares to the wind.
As it blows through the building from the back yard,
the curtains get big bellies, the blinds clank,
the flagpole rope flaps
across the strait, under the bridge, through town
nothing compares.
So, in the springtime, I dream of an autumn storm,
how it knocks down trees and scaffolds,
tears off roofs, nothing compares.
Did you read about the woman who walked her dog on a bridge?
It swooped her into the river, she drowned, I would have liked
to see that, nothing compares.
I've been wondering why
you come here, with your child,
your mother disappeared a long time ago, now she floats
on a calm sea, calm the whites of her eyes.
She doesn't know you anymore.

The Day's Bag

The day has a bag with plenty of room
for spittle and chewed bits of bread,
    mastications, swallowings, blinkings and winkings,
many bagfuls of yawns, borborygmi, quiet
leakings, talk, murmurs, whispers,
    glances at ice floes and open water
where the wake of a motor boat divides wave from wave
and a lone merganser drills its way
    all the way down to the bottom silt,
smoke rises from the power station's stack, and all that, too,
fits into the day's bag, church spires and containers,
    the giggle hidden in a child's neck and armpits,
the grinding of sand, the microwave's beep,
the clink of spoons, the clatter of cups, the cheating,
    the staring at the ceiling's flaking stucco,
the putting of arms around, the crawling, the sending
of messages, the reading, all fits
    into the day's bag, and there's room for more ...

But time is a mouse and keeps gnawing,
comes out of its hole in the evening
    and ties up the bag with a string,
carries it downstairs to the basement
as if it were full of cheese and oatmeal,
    date gateaux and braised beef that melts in the mouth,
the haste of that mouse carries the day's bag
from the basement on to the escalator to the subway tunnel
    down among the arriving and departing trains
and from there on down on the elevator to a mine shaft
hefting, heaving and pushing it
    even farther down along a ventilation shaft,

    splash, into the river of forgetfulness.

The Mole

Only now do I have time to reply, forgive the delay.
My son stole my pension money and took off to Tallinn,
don't worry, I'll manage, in a tin box under a rock
sleeps a rolled-up bill like a fallen paper soldier.
After he left I climbed up here to my cache and watched
how a mole appeared out from under the morning shadows
and charged at tremendous speed across the ice,
a small wingless airplane on its runway,
and it was just too bad that the wind
pushed it toward a hole in the ice.

STILL

The sea raises its hat of foam,
        a gentleman, the sea, the Baltic,
sleeps in its basin, eyes closed,
while the nets, the networks, the surface tension
        are still awake,
carries on its back ships, night clubs,
bits of planks, mussels and acorns,
        the water's green forest,

and the forest covers with its needles
thresholds, graves, flowerbeds,
        covers the early frost,
pulls a green sweater
        from behind its neck over its face
from Norway's fjords all the way to Vladivostok,

and still, still they hurt, the star nails
        in the palms of space,
bleed their light on the headland, the islands,
        the bayshore
on the harbor built on the cape and the church,
seized by the cold and vertigo,
        the street staggers, emptied by night,
        scintillates, sells advertisements,

and who wrote on the sidewalk
        Mari, I love ya!

does he live up there
        among the treetops,
does he stand by the window
        looking down, down here
at the loving couples, the maples,
the strip of park between buildings,

glowing under the streetlights,
        licking us
        with a tongue of sap

AT A BUILDING SITE

Is it an old folk's home they're building here?
I'm asking because I think it is good
that one doesn't have to move far,
and you look as if you knew
the answers to all questions,
sitting there, a child in your lap, gazing at a crane.
Boy, it goes up fast, and can he talk already?
My son always sat on the white couch,
dressed in green on a white couch,
one could hear the grass growing from his fingertips,
you couldn't look at it, and when you looked,
that spot was already empty.

It's All Different with Penguins

On their migration across the glaciers
the last penguins will be the first,
          and, like the Nazarene,
they allow the children to come to them
and let all of them be themselves, even those
          whom marriage does not suit.
No one needs to be a mate of darkness and carry
          an iceberg the size of the national bank,

     for the heavy and the light are equitably shared.

Thus, dear readers, if you are penguins,
thank your lucky stars and bless this
          freezing outpost.

(Blesséd be the ice under our feet! Benedictus!)

HALF WOOD

we are two and the leaves cover us
we are two and the roots take hold in us
you eat half the clouds, I eat the other half
you loosen half the soil, I the other half
when you die, I become a dog and howl
your ghost howls half of the howling
blinded by grief your ghost steps on a nail
it trots half of my run on its painful foot
and half of my paw is inflamed in my half
and half my grief glows as coals under your skin
and I turn the other half of my other cheek to death and say
not blind but having seen too much which means the same
    thing and say:
we are two for the sake of one half
from the half of this side to the half of the far side
like the one who watches impatiently
like the one whose song the trees run to listen to
like the one half of whom sings and the other half listens
of which half is two in which birds sit
as they sit in us and peck holes into us

ANNI SUMARI

~

FINLAND
TRANSLATED BY SARKA HANTULA

AUTOBIOGRAPHY

Without a touch of drama
the moon waxes and wanes.
I want to know what it means when the noise dies.
I want to know what it means to escape problems.
I want to know what it means to eat dirt
and to swallow your own tongue.
I want to know what 'a soul' means.
When the surface water in the lake is warmer than the air
fairies emerge.
The same happens above asphalt in the same circumstances.
I want to know what it means to watch problems disappear,
to throw yourself in front of a train? Ardently,
this minute! I want to know
what disappearance means,
assuagement, oblivion, abatement.

All the horror and death in the unknown
waters, battlefields, birth beds,
how it all subsides, abates, until
it's hard to believe, although you know —
hard to believe, although you can see it
gilded, engraved in marble —
hard to believe it has existed, that 'they'
felt the horror and death;
that 'he' or 'she' felt it; that 'we' did

in the waters, fields, beds
there is no other horror or death than
mine, mine, until it abates.
Autobiography
is the right word
to describe it
there is no other word
to describe it

The brain makes no distinction between
seeing, doing and imagination,
that's why creative visualization is so effective.
Follow the leader.
But the world is a mirror, if he goes right
you must go left.

A glimpse of the blue sky.
A glimpse of Picasso at work,
a glimpse of falling trash cans
and a smiling buddha in the hook of the crane.
Focus on guts that are flowing out,
that keep on flowing and sharpening.
Consciousness doesn't stream, it disrupts, cuts.
Shifts narrators, shifts rhythms.
Shifts perspectives, times, places from
one logic to another.

Compassionate, you know
horror and death as if you owned them.
Blazed, you watch
those who have lost everything,
who keep losing right and left,
who never succeed in anything
who are always plotted against
who are required to do the impossible,
who are being worn out, pushed aside,
who are chased, forced to escape

who have to trust, because there's no choice,
to passionately love no thing, the smallest
gesture, compliment, second-hand knowledge,
those who had barely caught their breath
when it was already too late
and who can now do nothing but
gape and radiate and yell:
"More! More! More!"

Gravitational farce of attraction that links
the inhabitants of the blue planet to each other,
to the serene, undulating golf course.
I deliberately forget all mountains —
the mountain, the hairy chest of a macho,
and the chapel on the hillside basking in the sun
like a golden pendant around his neck.

I can't believe my eyes,
and I find it even harder to believe God's speech.
Besides, the only god I've seen
abides in art. I just entered
the world, it wasn't too long ago,
if I were a horse or a dog, I'd be dead already,
in the human form, I dropped into the turbid
bellowing river, forced myself through
the entrance to the cave, I modified myself
to take my place in the jigsaw puzzle, I came up
to the expectations of the creators, I even adapted
myself to feel the martyrs' pain completely devoid
of the survival instinct, not a sound is heard
from the catacombs,
and look: here
I am.

A human being raises his hands in the air
when the road opens before him.
You'll come and see, gradually your own limbs,

your parts will tell you they aren't
what they were promised to be on Day One:
the lips aren't moist after all, soft, suckling,
the labia aren't moist, soft, suckling,
your forehead isn't high, arching, inquisitive,
the eyebrows aren't high, arching, inquisitive,
nor the eyes, the eyes — under the low forehead
are nothing to write home about.
What do Timur Lenk Gorge,
the Schönberg Chorus of Vienna and
the carousels of Bordeaux have in common?
I have seen or heard them,
perceived, sensed, heard them spoken of,
I'll take them with me. Autobiography
is the right word —

and the readers who have ventured
to talk to me, autobiography —
a childhood friend writes to me from prison
and wonders if I really am not interested
in knowing what has become of him?
A schoolmate writes from a mental hospital,
warmly, with good will, giving her best:
*"Jesus will be available at Helsinki Academic Bookstore
in 2006, in case you want to see Him.
Take care that in 2017
you won't be living in Southern Finland,
because it will be flooded with sea water."*

Ground beef. We are all
ground beef.
This insight is from my father.
When I was a child, he told me not to go
to the road where cars run over children and they
become ground beef. I believed it,
but my own conviction is that
we are ground beef all the time, we consist

of death, I'm the nearest direct
garbage chute to hell, I stink of decaying
ground beef, my brains are a certain amount
of ground beef, amazing how enjoyable
ground beef can be.
When I was the age of
the Crucified One, I thought I'd reached
the full age of a human being, at least metaphorically,
as well as averagely, generally historically —
from this day forth everything is luxury.
Extravagance. Years go to the left from the origin.
As if ground beef were being mystically edified,
the further behind the best-by date is left.
The more, the longer
you stand in the middle of the road
and a truck never comes.
Fiction comes
last, comes
and stays definitive.
The bottom line settles everything,
autobiography is
the right word.

FETE

The park's dark-green evening dress,
the soft sleeve, the tunnel —
the avenue we walk along.
We feel our way inside the sleeve
like a strange arm searching for light.
A pliant, longing arm of a strange body.

We listen to the sounds of the night, sawing, tapping,
hammering in the bushes.

Fete, we keep whispering
the password to each other.
This is a fete.
Cannot decline the invitation.
Cannot even leave the room,
the fete is about to begin.
No time to go back home
before the fete starts anew
in the middle of the road.

Seagulls shine on the lawn —
bird shit on the wet, black statue.
You have found people of your own kind, your look-alikes,
carved out of the same coffin.
Black boats float under their eyes, too.
They, too, believe that the spring will come again,
every instant will start a fete.

Skyrockets explode outward from their own core,
rockets bring something distant close to us
and then explode it, explode your face.
Exactly the right experience for a fete,
isn't it, you can imagine something changing.
The celebrants like the Furies,
the Erinyes, exude confetti, empty bottles.

Your image on the surface of the water:
it is you, but you are not it.
The stone wall crumbles, dissolves in the water
sculpted out of darkness.

Lamps of three colors light up
in the park: red, blue and purple.
The sea in some places so deep
that it swells like black chewing gum,
a black rubber raft slips into your ear.
Sand rustles into your ear,
the hourglass of your head.
The nose casts a long shadow
as if your face were a sundial,
a sundial in the dark night.

Someone slams a red clown nose
right in the middle of your face,
you swing around to look.
The Furies dance, waddling
ceremoniously, unintentionally comic,
holding up their hems in the whirl,
quiet in the accompanying currents.

Tell me what the celebrants'
abandoned kids said
when they passed you running
and shouting bang bang bang.
Did they wish to comment on something?
Sounds grow into a language for the children,
the language is a great death rider on its motorbike,
driving in a circle in a ball-shaped cage.

Do you already know everybody at this fete?
Names float around like flags in a stream.
Names drift among garbage scows.

Names are collected on a tray like disposable plastic cups
and eventually thrown away.

Where the trees end,
where the avenue ends,
a blind arm protrudes from the sleeve.
The fete is over
before it even began,
we lose our way in the unobstructed darkness —
into the lime white painted darkness.

THE SCENT OF LILIES OF THE VALLEY

I

Wassily lives in Berlin
he's a charming boy, a pain in the ass,
a wise, sensitive, experienced man, a good
poet, completely self-absorbed,
even his poems manifest the most blatant use of
the first person singular I've ever seen,
he's good-hearted, the only one
to whom I've ever said: Brother.
He's drunk his big nose red
smoked his teeth yellow,
an amazing lover, restless, irritating.
Wants to be looked after
but not watched over, he'd rather say
I *like you* three times than I *love you* once.
Wassily may live in Berlin
but he changes countries and girlfriends like shirts,
that is, not too often, *don't worry I know*
we'll break some borders together.

I'm alone and I love you
most warmly, deeply, tenderly.
I just can't help it, it's mainly
because of the long distance
but also because of you, you never
gave me a choice, I had to
develop the purest, most unselfish
love to survive in these conditions.
You're the one who gets me to
place the bones of my fingers together and pray,
for not very much, and express my gratitude, for getting it —
you're the one who makes it happen, and that
Weeping Madonna with her harnessed arms,
her I really understand.

In your place in the emptiness, there exists
some life of your size, your shape, your appearance.
Last night I hired a prostitute
who gently took care of me with all
possible devices, she claimed
she hadn't done that to a woman before,
she thought it was really funny, she giggled,
I liked her very much, her and
her rubber suit, I wish you'd been there.
Now I remember what Peter Zilahy said
to me: "*You* are suffering like hell."

You're no different from anyone else.
No doubt the human race as such
is the most diabolical trash
rambling, wandering on earth, so it's quite
enough that we just exist — it's enough,
my angel. And you shouldn't fear
self-consciousness, or hubris: you'll pay for it,
Do not tremble. You will pay for it.

Good morning, headache,
did you sleep well?
What would you like for breakfast,
my burden, my yoke?
I do understand that you don't love me,
I wouldn't love me either if I were someone else.
On the other hand we love another person
just because they are not us,
and then we say:
I've never met anyone else to whom
I would've wanted to say:
My kindred, my brother, my lover.

I look at you like a turbot from a hole in the ice,
a blunt hook in the middle of my flat face:
what the fuck does it have to do with us
what I've written about you and me!

I don't know what to say.
Your indifference would
upset a saint.
All I know is that you were being lavish.
The dawns collapse before me
like clock towers.
The lungs are hissing
and flying to the sky like
a runaway balloon, today the machines
are working even worse than
yesterday, the face of the moon reflects
the pale faces of the mourners.
The hands, the mistake-making
hands, the boats gently sweep the muddy flesh
of the river bottom, Wassily's dirty, boyish face.
Irrational tenderness, passion, obsession —
the primal cry of a bird.
Connected to the respirator and all those tubes
the body artificially kept alive
is twitching comically.
The compliant palms of the boats,
the compliant irons in their racks on the river.
The Iron Virgin. The rain taps absent-mindedly
but imperiously against my umbrella. Do it
do it do it do it.

And again you don't want
to crucify me on your bed.
You're angry because I've written
about you! After a few enraged
sentences you spit on my face.
I'm infuriated: Yes! I have written
about you! And I will write more!
Ten love poems for each slap, a hundred
for spitting! Love has a high price —

On the other hand all the shit
a poet has to lay her hands on
might turn to gold.
I don't mind having a marriage of convenience
I just wanted you to fall in love with me
as madly as irrationally as I fell in love
with you, that you would think as madly as me
that we'd be equal in insanity,
it wasn't any worse than that I hoped for us.

II

When, where then,
where will I see you next,
where will we set up our squeesary? lovallary?
where, against my chest? where, under the leaves?
Between my ears. Between my legs, against the perineum.
On plantain leaves. Between the palms of my hands. On my back.
The burden, a taste in my mouth. The night, black and white
like the debates of these scholars. We'll sleep
on an air mattress. I'll protect you
with a pearly shield and I won't sleep, the legs of sleep
won't carry me. A flute breathes whistling somewhere
and girls are being escorted home to be locked up.
In which rentery, which dancery
can I invite you to the next waltz?
I wonder where you poor thing will eventually die?
Which ailment, illness, which grief
will shut you up? Will you die happy,
with your boots on, or alone swallowed by the night?
You know that outside art, absurdity is not art
(to hell with me, I'm dying too)
Where, outside of what?

I'm comforting a child who doesn't understand
a word of my language, only
the head in my lap, a heavy weight
with which love is weighed. Your head
wouldn't be safer
even in a shark's maw

I sleep with the kings of Mesopotamia,
not with you, — ancient stars are twinkling in my night.
To the one I met: It's sad that you were born,
forced to live here, bound to die,
regardless of the abundance of beautiful things.
Meeting you was sad, because I can't get
enough of you and we'll have
to separate. Hopes that were never fulfilled,
you know all that — should we grieve and
miss our over-scaled hopes?
I'm happy with you, I mean
that the happy moments will push the unhappy ones
overboard, more cruelly than you would expect of happiness.
Should I be afraid of the future
because I know how easily things go
wrong, beside themselves, and we break, every time
these buckets clack against each other —
should I be on the alert for encounters at the well,
at the abyss filled with drinking water?

It's strangely uncomfortable to love, the world
becomes so small and the shadow remains,
the awareness that love won't last forever,
the clouds are already gathering, the shadow on the snow
is sometimes turquoise sometimes pink,
with a royal glow but it's still a shadow
the day will come when your cruelty will change
into cruelty of ordinary, boring, thoroughly-read,
spent people.

To the Sleeping One: I know you're alive
because life is panting and shivering inside you.
One hand is clenching a tissue,
the other holding the dick, my precious prince
is scared, holding death.
I complain about the sluggishness of divine mills.
The painstakingly acquired rewards
have experienced a metamorphosis, leaf gold
has peeled off, disappointment has limped across
the mosaic faces on the floor in thousands of sandals,
worn them out, unrecognizable.

Violence and self-control
show on our faces
like the right and left eye.
Everything is roaring, glasses flying in the air
brimming with crimson liquid,
as if someone were juggling them carelessly in his hands,
slow trays, sleepwalkers, are wandering in the air
at breast height, even a fork and a knife
dancing the schottische above a sandwich and
no sign gives away the presence of human beings.
There's a harness lounging in the corner. A woman's harness.
Someone showed up and turned into air. Air.
The same way as we, my cruel friend,
after we've got up from the red-hot gridiron,
the bed of hell the corners of which
are burning with germ-white flames,
we fall down in the forest ditch and crush
with our foreheads the fragrant lilies of the valley
whose lovely scent we then smell?

MARKKU PAASONEN

~

FINLAND
TRANSLATED BY RANYA &
MARKKU PAASONEN

I COULD TELL YOU

I could sink my hand into the entrails of a mechanical bird and lift a half-digested story into daylight. I could tell you about a city that awoke one day from a thousand-year coma and was a feeling machine, a cement brain floating on clay and swamp water. I could tell you about a city that fell in love with a boy from the Chinese quarter so that it had cameras follow and observe him unremittingly, a city that languished because it couldn't be a human being. But because life is not in the events but in the language that enfolds them, that folds and unfolds like an ample overcoat, a body sweating from its pores, because life is not in the events, I won't tell you anything. I find it more entertaining to wander about among junk, under collapsing eaves, to watch the stop lights twinkling in a distant street, to ponder on what life there could be like, in the fleeing speed, elsewhere, elsewhere. Look at this heap of wood and plastic, I would say, if I didn't know that you have nothing but a piece of paper before your eyes. Look what a marvelous diversity of species it conceals! Not to mention the reflections in the slush: if you reach out far enough you might catch a glimpse of the upper floors. The people living there sometimes even get to see the sky. For us, on the other hand, there are only the reflections. I could grab the light by its hair and pull it down here as it speeds past by its limousine, but I find it more entertaining to wrap you in the tatters of sentences, in the folds of words, in recycled light.

Disappearance I

I knew a man who searched for the city in his body. He showed me lymph nodes and cells gone wild. The system is turning against itself, he said. A year later he was swinging in the wind. The city buried its poor so well that soon they were arriving from every continent. One weaker than the other, they were sleeping in the market squares, in churches, thousands of wingless doves. Had they been given wings, they would have covered the sky, I thought, and a black cloud floated past my eyes, the cloud of thought. I was so deep in the dying city that I didn't notice the funeral car. It's not here for us yet, the Colombian said, it's here for the Moroccans. He knew the dead had the best view. They lived on the mountain and looked over the roofs. If you look down from the mountain, he said, the houses will remind you of gravestones. They live on Zeus' mountain, I concluded, but the mountain disappeared. My work is slow these days; I recover things from disappearance. By the time I recover one, two have disappeared. My accounts are precise. Therefore I don't count.

DISAPPEARANCE II

I met a friend who had lost his body. He was transparent and light. He spoke across the ocean. He enjoyed immaterial meetings. This worried me. I wanted to keep my shadow. I wanted to feel the ailments of my body. I told that to him. He said that the question of truth is not a simple one. Such virtual babble! I took my leave of him. I shuffled through a suburb that squirmed like an electric-shock patient. There were fires on the road-side. They were the souls of the homeless. Just then I felt the frost in my bones. I sensed the asthmatic respiration of the city. Miserable excuses! Now I honestly want to tell you only about what happened one evening in June: I was enveloped by a moment of disappearance. A glorious moment of disappearance! Even I, myself, don't understand: nothing disappeared. Except the clouds. Hah! Clouds! Ridiculous! We march toward a great soufflé. Here he comes, the prophet of the Judgement Day, they say, as I enter the dining-room. Do sit at the table before it disappears! How could they possibly understand? How could I produce evidence when everything that hasn't yet disappeared is here: a few translucent hallucinations...

METAMORPHOSIS

Why do people no longer see flowers dripping with blood, or daughters transformed into trees? You see what you believe. I look across the street into the park; I am acquainted with the sparrows and their mites, the feather-passengers. Under the bark I see veins through which water carries nutrients to the leaves; I hear the cells and membranes through which liquids trickle; I know the protons and the electrons, one system within the other resembling the dance of the planets in the court of the sun. Today, I am the Sun King. I stand in the middle of the park, I stretch my hands toward the sky and dig my feet deep into the ground. Arboreal heavens arch over me. The green is for me. The white lead willow. Like a monstrous oxidized wheel they turn around the axis I am. Slowly, from the past, the moss-covered machine quarries ore, petrified leaves, the forefather of the maple. Finally it plunges its scoop into the sediment in which history is being conceived from tales, and that's when a tree oozing with myrrh is lifted from the underground, a tree which is a girl, and a flower whose red petals are droplets.

FALLING

As I run my fingers over the keyboard and write this sentence, a man spreads his wings and steps over the eaves of the house across the street. It is not a coincidence. I look him in the eye as he falls, I see that he collapses like an exhausted star. He flutters his feathers, but time is a malicious cyst in his side. It weighs him downward, and he falls through narrow rooms, through the clink a knife left on a plate, through shores where he bathed only in a dream, through the city whose kilometers his feet know well. I look him in the eye as he falls, and I collapse: I see myself. My fingers fall off the keyboard, and I fall toward the street full of traces my life has left behind. Everything I have experienced weighs me downward, and that of which I know nothing weighs even more, for it has attached a plummet to me. Ten meters above the ground, the man falls through a doctor's reception room, grabs an X-ray from on top of the desk and realizes that the disease which will kill him is shaped like the map of the city whose street he will fall on a fraction of a second later.

I am Waiting

for knowledge in which to drown, in which to swim in every direction of the sea, in which a sea bottom mountain will stir, and when the trembling begins, it will begin slowly; the beginning will last for years and intensify even when you would no longer believe it possible; it will turn into a dance in which things scrape their skin, break their joints, rotate, hallucinate, before the tremors begin, and when they begin, they will begin with might, because they will have been charged with two or twenty years of expectation, months of vigilance, impatience and devotion; they will come with arms of a starfish on which plankton, clams and elementary life-forms will hang; they will drag with them scrap-iron and deck-chairs that will have clung to them during the journey over the sea, they will come foaming at the jaws, they will keep on coming even when you would no longer believe it possible; they will keep on for so many weeks that you'd seriously begin to believe they'll never end, and when they do end, joy, disbelief and dismay will follow because they will have ended, languor will follow, from which you would never expect to awake, and when at last you find the courage to look at the destruction they have caused, you'd wish that such knowledge will never exist again, and in that hope you'd begin to rebuild life from splinters, fearing that such knowledge will never exist again.

THE BOOK

Every day, I write an amorphous book. It is so full of turmoil, so bloody, that it seems to lack form altogether. Mites nest in its adhesive bindings, and when opened, the book hurls its leaves around the room. Letters change places, and it is quite impossible to read the words. If a lucid thought makes an appearance on a page of the book, an ink blot soon falls on it and corrodes it. If you stop paying attention, even for a moment, speculative beings will rise from the gloom of the letters and from the bogholes of ink; they are creatures of spirit and matter, of fire and water, and of both sexes, simultaneously. They spread their conceptual membranes for people to see, and ask for money in return. If they don't get paid, they escape from the book and rush out onto the street to shoot at anyone within eyeshot. They raid a gas station and turn the gas pumps into flame-throwers; in that jet of fire, they dance an obscene dance to the gods they are. They copulate and suddenly a terrible tragedy is conceived, a tragedy which would never fit into any book and about which I must therefore keep silent. When they tire of playing havoc, they break into my home and tie me to a chair. They torture me all night by reciting the names of their predecessors. That's when I think they're nothing but form, they know life only by name, and I burst into genuine literary tears.

The Machine

A machine, enormous as a brain, hums incessantly beneath the roofs of the pale little town. That's why the streets are empty and gray, as if sleep had been driven away, or perhaps the machine even rations sleep. It offers its udders to the inhabitants, and they rush to suckle, like calves they hang on to the nipples from morning till night. I see with my own eyes that the machine is no oil-dripping monster of former times. It doesn't look like a machine at all. No flywheels the height of houses, no transmission belts, no gears wearing each other away. Nothing romantic: no rusty springs growing out of the bowels of the earth. And yet, if you take a closer look, you can distinguish archaic parts among the modern ones: the scheming of animals, the mechanisms of war. I'm new in town, I search for the operator of the machine until I'm told that those offices were done away with years ago. I can't but marvel at how splendidly everything has been organized! It all works by itself: the machine blows power into its cavities and starts up; its lungs swell, and it creates a fiction which people enter. Everyone here carves his own destiny, I'm told. The machine makes sure everyone gets what he wants provided he only wants the right things at the right time. And hangs on to the udders! Those who loosen their gums from the nipples and allow their teeth to grow, have only their own stupidity to blame. I'm told that the machine's function is to pray. Incessantly it prays to itself.

A LANDSCAPE

What's the use of an artist who doesn't paint landscapes? Always the same question. So I primed a canvas and began to look for the horizon. I examined the joint of a pipe and a valve and waited for the sun, its dull face tarnished by wisdom. Only a sunflower hung above the fuses, a lump with its petals torn off, its scattering seeds rattling on the roof of the shack. The construction workers collected the seeds and rubbed them into their shoulders. That's why they were tanned and strong as if the earth had pumped the power of the bedrock into them. One of them gave me a push with the flat of his hand, and I spun round: the shack, the sheep-fold, the water-pipe, the barrels; the shack, the sheep-fold, the water-pipe, the barrels. They did it for my benefit; an arrangement such as this obviously provided me with the best opportunity to examine the landscape in the middle of which I was. Shack, sheep-fold, water-pipe, barrels. Shack, sheep-fold, water-pipe, barrels. They were doing the work of nature, continuing what the sun had begun millions of years ago, but on every round I go further back into the past: the shack, the sheep-fold, the water-pipe, the barrels flash past me again, again, just like before, only faster. Every now and then as I spin round I catch a glimpse of the horizon; it is dirty and scaly, and still there is nothing above it.

Freedom

I have seen the lips of the Goddess of Freedom. I saw them in Paris at the Museum of Technology. Famous men such as Rousseau and Voltaire were there. They floated in tanks filled with green liquid. I saw them in Paris at the Museum of Technology. They were connected to wires and animated by electricity. They floated in tanks filled with green liquid. It was not a pleasant sight. They were connected to wires and animated by electricity. That enabled them to perform simple movements. It was not a pleasant sight: electricity made their hands and feet twitch. That enabled them to perform simple movements. They were swimming with stiff strokes. Electricity made their hands and feet twitch. I've never seen anything like it. They were swimming with stiff strokes, although the liquid flowed fast. I've never seen anything like it. Floating in the tanks there was motionless plankton, although the liquid flowed fast. Although fierce currents flung the great men about, floating in the tanks there was motionless plankton, enjoyed by the great men for nourishment. Although fierce currents flung the great men about, they were indispensable for freedom, enjoyed by the great men for nourishment. In the tank to the right of Voltaire there were two metal bars. They were indispensable for freedom; only the lips remained of the Goddess of Freedom. In the tank to the right of Voltaire there were two metal bars, to which they were attached. Only the lips remained of the Goddess of Freedom; they were moved by computer-controlled bars, to which they were attached. Although the lips were of human flesh, they were moved by computer-controlled bars. I couldn't see the operator of the computer. Although the lips were of human flesh, they spoke according to a mechanical pattern. I couldn't see the operator of the computer; the lips seemed to be moving of their own accord. They spoke according to a mechanical pattern, in which each sentence recurred with accuracy. The lips seemed to be moving of their own accord; the impression was probably a deliberate part of the show, in which each sentence recurred with accuracy, so that the speech would have a suggestive effect. The impression was probably a deliberate part of the show: the lips repeated "freedom..." "the right of every citizen..."

and "equal before the law…" so that the speech would have a suggestive effect. What an important message! The lips repeated "freedom…" "the right of every citizen…" and "equal before the law…" The speech made a great impression on me: What an important message! I exclaimed. The speech made a great impression on me. How wonderful everything is in Paris! I exclaimed. I will tell my children how wonderful everything is in Paris. I have seen the lips of the Goddess of Freedom! I will tell my children: Famous men such as Rousseau and Voltaire were there.

THE ELEVATOR

I could argue that I had to leave because the house was sinking. That according to the official notification, the cellars were half-submerged in the swamp, on which the house rested supported by wooden piles. Like a South Sea bungalow, except that there were no corals. That would be just as true as any other explanation. I could tell you about the waste under the windows, the pipes cracking, the radioactivity. You'd understand. No, you wouldn't understand anything! But so be it: I left because the house was sinking. I had to climb. Rumor had it that people's feet stayed dry on the upper floors; that's the least one might expect in order to live a decent life. I opened the door to the staircase and waited for the elevator. The wooden structure was creaking; you should have heard how that house was complaining. The elevator shaft was gossiping with a sound coming from the outside, the notes of that music were attached to each other by wooden pegs. I was determined to step into the elevator, that relic of democracy, when the door opened and a dog was set on me. It was not as fanatical as its master who had made his way one floor downwards by then; it was content with sniffing my trouser leg. I have always been on good terms with dogs because I've never owned a dog. Fancy owning a living creature! I'm more inclined to say that I've been owned, but that's a different story, the present one has got entangled with the elevator cables and is waiting to be lifted. Who wouldn't be? The stairs would certainly have been a better choice, not so technical, and I don't even know whether you'd understand if I tried to explain the horror I feel toward stairs, as if I were climbing vertebrae. Besides, the rich slip bodilessly into their apartments, they have not had to wander about in the vascular system of the house, lean against its moldy backbone and catch their breath. As the elevator didn't show up, I started to suspect that new instructions had been issued, of which they had forgotten to inform me; I lived, after all, behind a rather humble door. The gate stayed closed and the shaft hummed in emptiness, a direct connection between the upper and the lower circle. Its emptiness was a necessary condition of its directness. I stuck my head between the bars of the gate in order to see deeper, I wanted to know if there was any truth in the rumor about the house falling into decay. But that doesn't matter any more. The rumor has already done the job, it has helped me to tell a story which won't elevate you in the least. Not in the least! Where do you think you're going anyway?

PÄR HANSSON

~

SWEDEN
TRANSLATED BY RIKA LESSER

FROM THIS DIRECTION I CAN SEE
the moon over the hockey rink's corrugated metal
over the soccer field's wide-open spaces
I move into the penalty area thinking of me
that I am you when I am not myself
and when there's a rush like a giveaway
above us the images my brain is a landslide
a sacrifice and a faith
a dead cow but not a homecoming
I think of us as a harvest of losses
a weeping under our arms and a
broom of grain that burns in spirals
when I run across the field
running and running

HOUSES

sure I can walk here in that which has
always been mine gave birth to and nourished me
calmly go for a walk here are single family homes
the white fences the hedges the stuccowork houses
have eyes that look at me

●

inside families are eating their meals
their love burning slowly emits
a weak sheen over the terrace and the trees
in the backyard my love is concentrated
a hard fruit in a closed hand

●

I can weep two three beverage crates
carbonated sunshine and garden furniture
a hammock a grandmother a grill full
of girls and stinging abuse if you
push me this far fredrik

●

shut up brother if I'm the one speaking now
if I'm the one sobbing logs
and bright yellow barges logjam boats
half a childhood my mouth a line
along the ume river stefan

●

in a taxi along a river valley turning green
a variable wind ripples the water a taxi
accelerates and the nordic light presses
against your head when midsummer eve rages
past like powerful giddiness everything swirls
around my clenched fist

●

it is the river the field and the luck of the curlew
two red tractors harrow a sun and a moon
yes the maypole its garlands straight down
to hell white house trailers tacking and eating
everywhere toivo

●

rain if only I can reach a main road and follow
its shoulder the broken lines a leash
flashing trailer trucks in flaming yellow
light and the heart inside the jacket the hand on
the heart can I come home then henry

●

if I am the representative
for a region's frigid outdoor experiences
27 below at the age of 12 months ice-picked
up the galvanized spiral staircase
to my maturity

●

are the trees' colors scattered on
the ground black trash bags thrashing
in the wind lean your body all that is slack
against a fence for wild animals be lulled into a
dull metallic rest that impresses
a wire mesh pattern on the skin of your breast

Birches

I watch TV, I watch what is shown. A big, red wooden house is transported by tractor-trailer along the main street of a small town; the townspeople line the street and their gazes follow the route of the caterpillar. An elderly couple has sued the municipality because two birches on their lot have been cut down without their permission. The trees were in the way when the house was coming through. The trees blocked the house's advance and were sawed down by practiced hands. First closeup: The old woman's restrained weeping when she recounts how her own mother as a young woman planted the two birches. Second closeup: Her husband's feet, as if turned to stone, beside the stumps and the sawdust scattered in the grass. The house is transported through the market town of Vännäs; the street is lined with people. Men and women nod and chat, children eat candy and ice cream. It looks like a pageant. Like a string of heads in front of the burning forest. I see what I see. I see what is visible and sit very close to the TV screen, run my finger over the dry, dusty glass and try to distinguish the faces in the crowd.

TRANSFIGURATION

Death is a transfiguration for families. When a family member departs, a well is bored, a gap opens which allows the survivors to look one another far more seriously in the eye. Early one morning you assemble around this deeply bored well. A pail is attached to a long sturdy rope, the rope to a reel, you take turns cranking the handle and then let the pail, filled to the brim with water, go around. You hand over the heavy vessel, look one another in the eye. You drink this cool clear water by the liter.

This pertains not only to the immediate family in mourning, whose father has suffered a heart attack while he was out running laps. It also applies to the other families. Those who stand around in groups in a parking lot, dressed up, waiting for the bells to toll them into church. The men look at their cars some other way. They look at their cars with different eyes. The women look into their husbands' eyes. Their gazes almost coincide. And the children look at the trees, the cars, their mothers and fathers with entirely new, astonished eyes.

It is when you let a heart that is much too large just run: an internal explosion on a bicycle path between Vännäs and Vännäsby. A quick death before the body has even managed to hit the ground. Unable to feel the hardness of the ground one last time. Dying in the air. To remain hanging, half-finished, amid the thunderous pealing of the bells. But also the thundering of the bells in itself. The bells' own bronze-toned clang tolling the assembled, dressed-up, weeping families inside. The families that have never been more distinctly gathered. They see one another very clearly now. They stand clustered into small groups in front of their vehicles. It is early in the day. Their eyes are newly bored wells. Death is right in their midst, transfiguring and transfiguring.

GLITTER

The morning sun bestowed light and glitter over the river and the sparse forest in front of the river. On this morning people were suspended by cords from the trees behind our house. Children's bodies hung from the trees; they bore the heads of adults and the features of adults. Their faces were large and ripe like fruits, while their bodies were smaller, atrophied. I took note of that difference between the bodies and the heads.

The cords were secured under their arms, and their shoulders shot up toward their round cheeks. They hung as in harnesses and certain individuals smiled at me, tired smiles, as if they had recently been rescued from the sea or from the scene of an accident. Some of them I recognized, others not at all. But there they were before me, gathered up and real as a circle of friends. Behind them the sun poured its light over the water in the river, and now they all smiled at me and I no longer felt nervous.

I walked around under the tall birches and touched their dry bodies, their reddened cheeks, their feet like spears pointing toward the earth. I whistled a familiar tune, I imitated the wind and set everything I saw in motion. The children's dry hands swayed in the wind. The heavy heads of their parents swung and smiled. The body and the head and the space between them, gaping sunlight that gave and gave.

AGE

A person's age is a rusty cage hoisted up in a tree in a familiar courtyard. Up there sits this person, a boy, inhaling the scent of wet, newly mown grass, contemplating the view and attempting to turn everything to his advantage. He is given food, he does not go thirsty. And what happens happens for his sake. Everyone's thoughts are with him. Everyone's thoughts want to cut the grass and chop wood. Want to work with their bodies and make themselves elegant. Polish their nails, go to dinner parties, give the neighbor's children something to eat and drink. Thoughts that live in his head: That he is not himself. That he is mom and dad and their vertigo, their highest wish. A brilliant guy. Their spitting image hoisted up and moored. He sits in a rusty cage. It rains straight through. He rubs his body into the soot and rust to merge with the metal. In order to become one, as if poured in the same mold, to focus on the ground and coincide with his own age.

Five Flags

I

you are out wandering you come home late you come home early
you have been in the woods the woods exist you have seen things like bones like snow
you've seen the horse's head alive by your foot in the shimmering green moss
say the horse's head is alive at the foot of the vertical pine trees' beginning and end
say the sky in the animal's spherical eye disappears when it squints against the sidelight
you are out wandering you come home late you come home early
say this tell this to people the nostrils are trembling from the horse's smoke

II

all this exists snow bones and cloud-smoke exist in your eye turned this way
you are out running just to run returning home erect and bent
unfurl the flag and look at your friends when they see your flag from above
are your friends among all those reined-in faces that lose in your place
sew metal bands into these faces tape sew on bunches of nettles and grass-
hoppers' hind legs twine lilac-sinews together let beauty grow like a
doll of flesh let the doll fall apart and look something else fresh arises

III

certain passages are too narrow you must go another way discord
sometimes in the gravel people become invisible when the herd backs in
urge it on while waiting for the cloth to fall and the first clear star
a thousand small lamps to be lit in the warm cloth's dark-blue folds
not far away only a rustling tremor against the ribs the crown of the head
certain passages are too narrow you must go another way discord
self-driven toward the end no the herd goes first toward the day breaking

IV

the city is never far away when it hides in electric light
this is a tale you tell when the wall cools down you change sides
formerly the lid of light pollution hid the sack's cloth when it fell
now you lie on the floor while the stars drop threads toward your belly
the story for the child when the wall warms up the child falls back asleep
the city never far away hides in electric light and superstitions
reeks of exhaust fumes you are telling this by command of the thrush

V

a lamb in a barn a hasp and a lamp say the woods exist
in the distance between trees and within the word whitebeam beam yourself forth
if the liver is bigger than the heart say the word find the arrow and send
the arrow toward the liver's heart do you aim low now or are you just anxious
you are out running just to run coming back home erect and bent
let yourself be awakened kept awake and become the breast the neck the head
of the horse keep me awake alert and I'll become the face you ride

Lars Mikael Raattamaa

~

Sweden
Translated by Bill Coyle

Schumann's Cello Concerto in A minor, Opus 129

I.

Soon before surges just and so collides
But chills while reddening to coolness flows
Having been rung through three begins to be
Is touched and blended and grieves readily
Soon before foaming that grows darker rides
So soon now follows just which just now chose

II.

At light green-gray cold true and ostentatious
Which quaint around already thousand blue
An oboe-wet but very timely low
Toward silver raw above silk tangled through
Small soft in shadowed hard but slowly gracious
And soon as cello moistness makes leave now

III.

When by the window long the midnight day
And noises up the stairs soon and the nest
And the birch clearly not the pattern when
Our house constructed air and building waste
And the bow's keyhole light the motorway
Kristallbahnnacht and dead I now and then

LEGION

St. Bartholomew Night's Wormwood
has been left to ferment

That winter morning
in Skärholmen when I stood
before the nearly dead
with their frozen little souls
A line of green
overcoats, mittens, cloth
over a thick carpet
of money   It is memory; it is stamps
That night
yes, yes, it was something else
12 000 slaughtered Belgian pigs
hung to dry
along the E4
The aluminum scaffoldings'
dull ribs
stick through the backbones
while the winds
polish, dry the meat
The line shouts
other names
Vitrolles, Toulon, Orange...
Other languages
behind the silent languages
Skärholmen's white concrete is swept by woven snow
and the line goes in measured steps around itself
around or around

And St. Bartholomew Night's Wormwood
has been left to ferment

EVE

we should have stayed out on strike
it could have been a reason to survive
since the chromosomes
in the genetic braid were counted
and the number found to be too large
it was time to leave
all the cubic meters in the packed halls
filled with Birgitta and Isabell
filled with Heli and Helga
Sanna, Thomas and Knut

journey thus
to Happy Bollmora
that rolls in the bodies
in sundew
(we should have asked them at the office
—if that's the way you want it
then we can create you anew)

rest here in the crowded hedge
in the double mouth

wemoney

in the welight

LEILA KHALED

FOR THE PALESTINIAN FREE STATE

The weight of September creeps through
the peel again
The knife's way of opening
and the calm green veins
gather the particles together
to rules for a new game
Some are split
some are depicted in the cord: the braid; the gold
bone pipe
no, you're not allowed to see, not yet
Birthday presents
between the table legs
There they stand again this year   once again
the children are gathered in the mountains, almighty
children and chameleons that cautiously
chew on the truck's rubber tires   School crowd
from the hovering
biology chews
Peugeots, melons, tobacco
lady-like saliva
or is it maybe a way of playing
surely you can give the loom a rest
Black dogs from millennia old
families in the rain of splinters
Drops of meat under the table
and drops on the point of a pen
do you remember how beautiful Haifa looks from the mountain

ANABASIS

First sand, on top of that stones and furthest up a lid of
concrete,
Next to a rooted barnacle, to at last close the surface
wandered in into bubbles she and I try
to follow the arrows out of, no into the wreck of creation
where the grace of water rinses its underwater waves of granite
through our joint capsules   Further
as the hope and the bottom-dwelling owls there
between the blocks   and the eye-spiders that wait in the seaweed
diluted and expressionless deep-sea creatures in great nets
but first sand

Before the Sermon on the Mount

Coronary vessels; removed
with sterile steel
Rung reflexes and tissues
hover a millimeter
over the collapsible table
The gauge, which never
stops breathing, opens
toward the bodies of snow
The life wave ticks
A hare
set down beside the highway
like a disguised king
In the night soft steps
into the lump of clay
It is called Löwenström
but the name should have been Anckarström
The name should have been Anckarström
The name should have been Knight Templar Anckarström

The Names Distance Themselves

The children with distorted voices
open their sacks over
the swamp of leaves
The sign's text
between the trunks of elms
is smudged out by rain and weather
So the white wall is lit in Kavli's office
split by
the glass shadows
the fuzz of the surprises, the grown
water
there shine, shine and rotate
the name brands
between the forest and the trainyard
The children with the empty sacks
move without being seen
in the swamp
You can hear their wet
feet
You can hear how someone is felled
and lies there
They are not of a helping race
And while weeping is gathered
in split buckets
the names distance themselves
mycelia force their way
through
and cover the sleeping
while they sleep
Hospital green and hospital white
They wake are not many
a woman, maybe 30 years old
approximately 160 centimeters
wearing a thin
white jacket with a hood
and light green cotton pants,
out on the road, ahead of the bus, cycles

a lady around 50-55 years old
dark blue dress
The cycle is hand painted
purple and gold
The forest doesn't stretch
farther than to the playground
There it meets the red piles of bricks
(ring around the roses
a pocketful of neuroses)
No, it isn't really awake yet
Bus 144 isn't even half full when
it turns in toward Älvsjö station
The green grocers' stands are lying
on the ground
Children have been here, trails
of gasoline
and cloth wind
up the stairs, along
the ramp, over
the tracks
Some children
are laughing down on
the platform, some inside
the fence, by the shacks behind
the fairgrounds
(the shadows are green)
Leaflight   glass roof   night pennants
Here another forest begins
it isn't mine
Give it a name!

                / / /

flame; crash; news; punish; praise
ha-
ve

the orange color dies, an arrow on the bridge at Samarkand
erb area
ryan; sux; pix;
on the pillar under the bridge
chemistry; poms
the year's; rudy
gobi; fast; rene
in the corner råby road - turinge road
wau, written above chemistry
ha-
ve
gones, 35 turinge road
rent • • gobi on a lamp post
power
in the adjacent electrical cabinet
turinge road - the old huddinge road
number 459: news; flame
number 458a: have
smir
wonder
why • • nan
pinkie
at the video store south of south
the old huddinge road 439
at the intersection with the stigtomta road
ha-
ve
örby school
rabble; flame; avid
and on the electrical cabinet is a poster that
someone has tried to pull down
tonight one more/swedish woman will be raped/stop violence
against women
vote swed/
swedish democr/
under the poster: goose; nille

ha-
ve
on the bus hiuho
the old huddinge road 422
has sofie; teresa scratched in the glass
urbe
the old huddinge road 420a
ha-
ve
on the side of the house
the old huddinge road 409
the block the ball-bearing at
the corner ludgo road, is scratched
camilla; sara n anne; mazer; i luv boys
sara 4-ever
anna n sara
robin; jenny; i luv thomas
zandra
drop; diva; kenn
the block the flat tire
on the sign that shows the way to bandhagen; högdalen
crash; guts
ha-
ve
a black high-heeled ladies' shoe on
the sidewalk outside örby konsum
and on the other side of the thruway
is written chids
four times on four connected electrical cabinets
ha-
ve
on the other side - chids; bare; riox
örby glass, tosterö road 21
(the old q8)
stile; rudy; terz
kare; next
aux; site; ha

and on the metal eaves
kir; nox; taiwa
and farther away
fate; anus; glock, nan
roms; flame; rudy
grozier; riot; chids; gut
and in pink green and silver
rudy
god is gay
sara marie sofie and anne
on the noise barrier - sero; aux
it is the map given
the tunnel of leaves up to the road to örby castle
ha
-ve
rudy; rudy
the bus stop örby castle
titian; poled
the yellow star on örby castle
rudy
there are railings here
in the corner örby avenue - julita road
up on the cliff you can see all of stockholm
the markings on the transformer station
26 östberg heights is painted over
here begins the summer

No

schumann begins now:

a couple of lines about the houses in Bredäng, about the details of their facades, the space nearby, the square, no, but the winds carried Lake Mälaren in between there, such in the lovely, can't we, but the happiness in the houses in Bredäng, thus write, in the middle of the line, so can, no, there's sheet-metal under there, polished sheet-metal, sturdy like never before, noo

JÖRGEN LIND

~

SWEDEN
TRANSLATED BY RIKA LESSER

A Theory of Evolution (The United States of Amnesia):

I know nothing about birds, but when we get home something black is lying on the sun chair on the balcony. Unclear what it is, but it must have collided with the big window in the living room at some point during the last few weeks. Its beak a trifle open, its eyes closed. I pick up the dead body and set it in a hole out in the yard. (...) The smallest structures have weight. But you can never undergo variation and attain refinement. You can't be any sort of imitation. I have to make a real effort to believe this: no modulated cell clusters, no biosynthesis. I lie on top of you. Your sex against mine and we are with each other. Predators. We move. And if I open myself maybe you are there. We tremble. We break in two. Sometimes I think you are a stone. Now I know that you scatter, unfold, when you open me a person is there. Now it's audible, auricle and ventricle, weak as a second hand from another century. When I do not fall I will get to my feet. Now release. Now movement: we are each other, a unit, muscles. Maybe you are something else. The negatives dissolve completely. I touch your childhood. Your mother and father together in a whitewashed house. If you try to scream you are sucked into the gravitational field and vanish. Now we move. Move abruptly. I take your hand and touch your darkness. You press. I receive. Now tightening. Release. You come through. (...) I wake with a mariachi band in my brain and dance over to the dish rack. Out the window trees are still green. Smiles and rapture still precede grammar. Despair is still a long way off. Still is everything. Now and then still a heaping measure of fulfillment. Still a presentiment of grace. Still is still. (...) They are unmanageable. They are useless. They use us: building bridges, laying out road networks and cities. They transmit, stream past, fall apart. The rhythms of economies. Minimal, private ecstasies. Marginalia to new states and realms which none of them are. Feelings mistaken for fabrics, summer that contains winter, winter months transformed to years until the roof caves in. House sparrows are winched down through whirling snow by ingenious mechanisms of lacing. Louise Levander is dead. (...) Number one fell through a night on the outskirts of the illegible and became all those I attempt to write when I no longer know where to turn. Number two was one-third dream, one-third thirst, one-third the grave. A closed egg around its empty riddle. Number three: two feet at a 45-degree angle. The sofa was brown with a large floral pattern. I tried to touch one big toe,

but screamed that there was nothing that
could make me. Was never worthy of
number four, but moved closer as if it were
possible to stop thinking. Now I think
with my fingers and my sex: these eleven
nails that hold the body together. Che
tempo, che tempo, number five! From
time to time the road divides, but this
cannot be the crossroads marked on the
map. In any case we're headed in another
direction. Besides there are reports of
continuing rain in Pavia. Number six at
the traffic light. Neither forward nor
backward. Walks and walks, but never
comes out in the sun. Number seven calls
him Brahman. His name is Lars. Our
bodies became one and vanished. There
was no monsoon. There was haze and a
thermos of coffee somewhere outside Tjörn.
Number eight taught me reconciliation
with what allows us to fall. I will tell your
secret: during the day you are a fluttering
dannebrog, at night a stone at the edge of
the road. Tonight someone else will give
you a name. But tomorrow you will
disperse as soon as it is pronounced.
Number nine, I ask for forgiveness, but I
cannot stop writing about you. You are a
system of modules, your units extend all
the way into infinity. Sorry, number ten,
but your life has no weight. Synthesized
nature. The sack of my shadows. One
night I confused your arms with those
plastic tubes filled with light pulsating
with the bass in a discotheque in the
provinces. I don't want to see you ever
again. Number eleven: forgive me for this

hypothetical mapping. Everything is in motion. There are no contours I can force you into. You are constant erosion. Contraction. Expansion. Divine abstractions will also collapse, be reproduced and worshiped again. I shall not destroy you. (...) This collection of assertions could be a grammar for some kind of agenda. Energies allocated according to new distribution schemes. But I don't know. Something is pointing and whispering and blinking. We hear it when we come back. You can never be reduced to mere profit for another person. Here come the warm currents. (...) In two minutes it will be night. We own nothing here, the right of tenancy rests on an invisible foundation in the clouds. Traditionalizers. Duplicators. Here everything is set: the lindens along the canal which the rain has pushed up out of the earth. The child when we walk with her downtown. She stands and stares, stares and lingers as if there were a waiting, for a word, a form of address, in order to say something, a longing for something to long for. Your throat works. And if I do not possess love, what is the meaning of these proddings, the hand stroking the child's head, the words being forced out of me? Here come the warm currents. The asymmetries work with one another. But there are other structures. Days when I did not step outside the door. Food on the balcony. Canned goods, plastic packs, whatever. But now I'm able to move and want to reach out with my hands. What can I desire if I do not have love? I make

my approach. You will not push me away.
But writing about this is only giving a bad
rendition of some days in June. What
difference does it make what you and I do?
We surrender to one another. I am being
confused with a father. The child is a
different child. Louise Levander is dead. I
can't write this any other way. (...) Give
me an A for *Australopithecus anamensis*,
simple as a stone that thinks of you
somewhere far from here. Give me a B for
Basic Object, the knife that carves a C for
Chatwin, Bruce (1940-1999), 48 years on
this earth. Give me a D for Devon (not one
night without thunder and rain), an E for
Erosion, 550,000 cubic meters of gravel
that are flushed out to the delta. Give me
an F for Fossil, when you touch a shoulder
a few million years too late. Give me a G
for Gene Fluxes and the faces that circle
around them: H for Homo habilis in the
great Intellect that has never been. Give
me a J for the Jurassic, a K for the sound of
Cretaceous. Give me an L for Lucy where
she sits on her haunches by the riverbed,
opening her first oyster. Give me an M for
the Mammoth mass that remains inside
me. Give me an N for Neanderthal and I'll
say: *body*, you'll answer: *cool breeze*. Give
me an O for Ornithosuchus, a P for
Pleistocene: I love you, whatever it means.
Give me a Q for Quantity Q and a primordial
ripple: the number before one, as if displaced
in a mirror. Give me an R for Romany, an
S for Sanskrit: historically seen, no great
strides have been made in the realm of
sentiment. Give me a T for Triceratops,

where you move across the grass before disappearing among segments. Give me a U for Ulven, Tor (1953-1995), 41 years on this earth. Give me a V for a Vision of world order: I am only an ordinary stone that is speaking. Give me a W for WT 15000, who gets up and claps his hands. Give me an X for Xolotl, the underworld's slobbering seeing-eye dog who fetches bones for these 24-hour periods between two parentheses. Give me a Y for Ypsilon, mother-tree for cells and anti-cells, a Z for the Zero Universe. From alpha to omega, may they come streaming in endless warm currents. (...) I'm tired. So are you. We've been tired for three whole years. Some days are more like writing exercises than a marriage, you say. Two sleepwalkers who depend on each other. How much is really left of us. A few hundred grams of food. Yogurt. Rice cakes. The lamp we turn off at night. Begin again. Clear out the concepts of soul and the latest tire options. I never meet you however lost I am. You, you, you. The anxiety that comes in china-blue, electrical currents. (...) They vanish. A gradual dissolution. They become more and more transparent, hang in soft flakes, like something from Japan. Under lindens that are turning green one can find some specimens; only their nerves remain, like remnants of outmoded textiles. Simple gray nests that finally cease without one's being able precisely to state when. We move them. Take them with us when we go out. They are destroyed, burn up, are transformed to indecipherable dross. They break down with rampaging half-lives. They vanish with their small load of air and water. (...) *The light that soon goes out in a hollow with no furniture or windows. Maybe it's an air-raid shelter or a container at a rest-stop outside Mainau. Hurry up and write so we don't vanish: nicknames, slang, overheated pornography. But your fingers are swollen, powerless cavities, as if they worked in a sterile glass box in the Institute for Infectious Disease Control. Emaciated and exhausted you lick the moisture from the walls.* (...) Thrusting and giving way. We force ourselves, squeeze ourselves, rising and sinking, down into each other. Probes. Signals. In the clouds, into the blue. Whirling, empty open-plan offices. Modules for castles in the air, listed on the stock exchange. It falls. We too shall fall. We see it coming. Fiber optics for synthetic breath when we read the inscription "Beyond" on a gravestone near Bromma Church. (...) *It don't take a weathergirl to see where the wind is blowing.* We are hurled out into the sun or are dispersed in all directions. Something breaks down. I begin again. It starts completely unexpectedly, like an accident. The blank page, an impulse, a target area, a conjunction of hand and keyboard. A direction, a line, I follow it, as it develops, spreads and drifts, living, alive. We go over to the child and say her name. When I lay my hand on her head I must believe in an absolute symmetry. And everything begins anew. I can once again believe in the beauty of zero growth and abundant care. And if I were forced to continue to write this way to be able to maintain it, yes, then I would not hesitate. The keynote is wonder, the voice that asks and desires, your outstretched arm coming from deep inside the darkness. Here come the warm currents.

"Here come the warm currents / Här kommer de varma strömmarna" is Lind's translation of the title of Brian Eno's first solo album, Here Come the Warm Jets (1973).

"The United States of Amnesia" at the start of the poem and *"It don't take a weathergirl to see where the wind is blowing"* toward the end are both citations of the English musician and lyricist Robert Wyatt. The first is the title of a song on his LP Old Rottenhat (1985); the second is from *"Blues in Bob Minor"* on Shleep (1997).

A few minor changes have been made in the text of the original poem since its publication in the first Swedish edition.

Håkan Sandell

~

Sweden

Pigeons

Healthy metallic the pigeons
glisten in shadows of woods.
Fragile though richly so colored,
billowing shawls of pure silk.
Slender and vividly red their
claws are so perfectly female,
also exquisite on males.
Heart beats disguised by apparel,
welcome so lithely as snakes,
sea color high in the pine trees,
look for me after some decades.
Velvety sounds for the moment,
ringing on miniature tongues,
finding their greatness in memories.
Pigeons in sheltering spruces,
haziness turns into clearness,
in twilight the amber eyes piercing.
Also when lying there slain,
a falcon's remains in the glades,
unruly opal gray fragments
burdened by weights due to wind,
with temple-like forest surrounding.
Wings are mirrored in rivers,
embellish the light and the air.
Encountering you who condemned
polluted not copious greenery,
foliage that has in one's eye,

chased along allies and sidewalks,
scraping irregular circles
with feet that are bony deformities,
renders the picture of innocence,
well-rinsed in gray clustered grapes,
trampled alongside the street.
Traces as if made by Leonardo,
heels that have quickly retouched.
Soot blackened pigeons turn reddish,
openly obscene as in death.
Pigeons that ridiculously totter
on track from fodder to danger;
mocked and bedraggled clowns
assenting far beyond cowardice,
more locked than a candle's flame.
Still in the pigeon's blue loftiness,
cast in a statue's bold shadow,
or wings that are fully stretched
as Symbols of ethereal dreams,
the notion of once having
resided in a world that has value,
nourished by a forest's dominions.
Cynical minds will still claim that
they're just a pest and a vermin —
could pigeons by chance ever fly?
If you perhaps were to see how
sickly and ruffled they perch,
sullen in rubbish-filled gutters,
alongside their eggs are so putrid,
confronted you nakedly stand
in places where matt poetry glows
remembering all that is wasted.

TRANSLATED BY FINN PRINTZ-PÅHLSON

TIME AND SPACE

My time is now, my place is here,
the password long since been spoken —
no longer do I need to seek for it.
But as a wing will try to test its flight
my eye has difficulty finding focus.
It's injured in all kinds of ways,
by mediocre and unsightly things,
on cornered squares and in restricted space;
scrapes and sprains and hits the roof,
blinking slightly in its blackened eye
until it — bend now backwards! — rises up
and finds its freedom in a widened room
as if this eye had planned to annex it.
There is a limit to what one manages
of stuffiness and stifled breathing.
How easy to lose one's creative drive
and crouch despite the sky above does
incessantly generate new fresh frescoes
with clouds so airy white and monumental
that they only leave behind small traces
of the blue that inaugurated the place.
My eye must die in your apartments,
it's getting gray, the world is fading,
and only flashes in the lighter's flame,
the moment before the smoke's new grayness.
The ceiling's low, the cage is cramped;
a sudden glance, with nothing to lose.
It's a crime you know, to turn one's back
but I fled, to nature's lap,
to Irish rivers and Norwegian hills
and drowned myself in rapture wild;
the sound of jubilance, my head
was swept along on frothy waves.
But as rebellion's seeking in, and digs
its heels, or takes off into the woods,
it must loyally one day return to fight.
I'm all cracked up, but my nut is ripe,

it has brightened, sweet and golden,
its shell no longer needs to hold it.
I'm feeling what I've always felt,
how the forces that strive to unmake
exactly measure up to those that create,
and if there was to be a task for me,
it should be a one to fit a mold
of sorts around a gloomy void.
I bring the contours back to twilight,
from stubble blue I'd like to make
a color print so time preserves,
a weight for the floating, fillings
for the vacuous and hollow.
From these dreary quarters a draftsman
might now and then appear, although how rare,
who with a sharpened pencil point
can lend the skies a bold relief
and, line for line, recreate the space,
and where at dusk — and godlike —
the bright blue air fills in with ease.

TRANSLATED BY FINN PRINTZ-PÅHLSON

TO A CHILD TWO WEEKS OVERDUE

Pardon a complete stranger for pestering,
but if beauty, good will and love have ever
worn a human face, it must be your mother's.
She looks so welcoming I have to wonder
if you're not being unnecessarily skeptical.
You're expected, the white, tightly-stretched
blouse where the bra is struggling mightily
to restrain that swelling so as not to overwhelm one
with its friendly generosity ought to be enough.
But maybe she has a lazy-bones onboard, someone
who'd rather stay there in peace and quiet
in that crock pot's lovely, honeyed sweetness
and the magic potion of that rounded crucible
than come out in public, exposed and freezing?
The capsule like a sail, soft and flexible
vast as the whole world, though a mouse hole.
You stand upright — the sides soft as seashell —
and if you decide you want to lie down and rest
your mother holds you as in a swan's egg. You yourself
are the light where the nights tuck you into bed;
pale star — in ten light fingers
you sparkle, you spin, with head down.
Do you know the secret, just before you spring,
of the world that opens, are you able now,
in that inwardness where the red lips say nothing
to see that when your thin, silken hair
reaches the roughness of her golden brush
the sun and moon will be waiting for you there!
When you've tired of your container's marine
life and the sea swell's untroubled peace
in this, the most feminine of places, and finally
make up your mind to come out in a hurry
you're going to be proud, I know,
of this new being you find holding you.
And that you, despite it all, have come out of the night's
grip to horizons immeasurably broader
will be clear, and later, when you're squirming beside

your mother, as if nothing more than a drop
fallen from the nakedness of her hands or feet,
know that you once again, like a chameleon,
will find yourself in the unfamiliar body.
Brown-eyed, as if taken from the shell of the chestnut,
Or blue-eyed, trickled from the greater stream,
center of that milk-scented creation,
naked and newly hatched and perfect.
Stretched out from that arch where you reclined,
rolled out to full length from that fold of velvet,
you'll be greeted by an intimate admiration.
The rounded stomach and the little behind
fresh from the garden of roses sprung,
how ephemeral, like a cloud, yet how earthly you are.
Welcome, little night-guest, eyes still closed,
loosened from the heavens, rosy star;
like a crèche's Jesus, dreamy, illumined
twenty-pointed, perfect little human,
most wondrous, most beautiful, most linen-soft you,
with the lines of a wave and the skin of a flower.
Come now, come out from your rounded house
don't linger any longer in your corner, in the shadows.
Large in your loneliness, alone in your bowl,
crawl your way out of an outlived world.
The hold can no longer contain your journey
to awakening and the patient completion that waits.
But given how long you've already waited,
you'll probably climb, or so I imagine,
directly up in your mother's lap
and be able both to count and to comb your hair.
Your mom is going to do it all for you,
she already breathes your breath — and nursing?
the little leaves of your hands flutter
on their stems — I swear it — as your thirsty
mouth finds its sanctifying raspberry touchstone.
Like the necks of swans, your arms as you sling them,
thin and fair, around your mother

in a moment of mutual, mild seduction.
Come out for a while — you can always go in
again — I promise you, just like Aladdin
promised his reluctant djinn —
if that embrace doesn't meet with your satisfaction.
Come out, in any case, don't wait forever!
Come out in these years when your mother is young
and believes so hopefully in life's wonder
and that it still can transform everything.

TRANSLATED BY BILL COYLE

SOUL AFTER DEATH

"Now I see clearly that a warming sun
was my body to me and that the reverse darkness
of light's abstractions has chilled me through.
I miss the body, and the warmth of blood.
I miss my graying skin, and the daybreak's
cough, the arteries' refilling from the heart
in a strong flood through my autumn colors,
the tattoos as soft as on silken cloth.
In the aged body, in spite of it all
the remains of youth rejoiced in the present.
The shoulders were worth every bit as much as wings.
A seraphic shrine surrounded the pigskin.
The watch's miniature toy-world on the wrist
contained exhilarating depths in its hours,
the minutes shimmered more than the eternal stars.
I miss the brain's stability — a gem
of clarity, miss the rib-cage's breathing,
the sex's hardness, the muscles that tense
in strength, the blood streaming out to the hands
to turn around, then, as in the crucified man's,
and that the air of what is fine and old and transitory
is able to draw into the lungs once more.
Every scar a precious memory, abandoned,
now, with the wedding ring grown fast to the finger
and the body itself, so soon obliterated.
If I nevertheless, for one turn more,
were permitted to step out of the abstract and into
my earthly tabernacle, I long to go back
like the angel Gabriel to Mary's innocence,
to the old security of a point to hold fast to
when identity turns away, and in its absence
the empty space is flooded ecstatically."

TRANSLATED BY BILL COYLE

TONE HØDNEBØ

~

NORWAY
TRANSLATED BY ANTHONY BARNETT

O, MY LOVE, rest in my heart,
the weight of lovers,
the weight of loneliness drowns me.
I hear my own words
as if they were those of someone else
who talks of things that only I know,
of the one whom I loved.

I could be struck dead
and then begin to speak
as if a curse existed
making me my own enemy,
the one whom I loved.

I hear my own words,
O, rest in my heart, my love
for without this openheartedness
you are lost in the shades' abyss,
you, the only one whom I loved.

GLOBE

You whirl me around
like a sun
and hocus-pocus
when I am in that mood
no one can keep me quiet

For it will be held against you
something you cannot see,
a weight in all that can talk,
think and be

and nowhere outside
you can flee to and slip away
so the world can be silent.

FOR EVERYTHING THERE IS a reverse trajectory
you turned round,
and the blind followed you,
you walked while you slept
and afterwards someone removed
your hands from your eyes.

As though you had hidden yourself
and wanted to be the last one found.

The hedge grows
and we lie down to sleep
so that the unexpected shall appear,
and the unfamiliar shall happen,
a wall from which thorns fall,
and roses bore through the ground
to where there is a gate
but you have no idea where it leads,
only that the curse shall end
should the dream come to the sleeper
and promises be fulfilled.

WHEN YOU COME HOME you dream
you are walking home, it's snowing, and you dream
it's snowing, the wood is murky, and you want to run
back

to where the light sifts
out through the high windows onto the snow.
Under the door a note with a message:
you shall find the others

in another dream.
A door swings open, and your father
enters to tell you are grown up,
you almost nod

for you sleep sweetly, because
you can no longer distinguish the dream from
your own breathing.

WILL THE DEAD teach you how the river runs
how the sun shines on the other side
of the sun,

and how the nightingale sings in her sleep,
how the storm calls you to go out,
hammering on the windows to get in.

Will the living teach you
that no one is closer
than the one you are thinking of,

and how the wind can never be a wind,
only locked into a storm,
and no sun more distant.

Your shadow is full of life
closer than on the page before you,
and in the erasing blood that keeps you alive.

So alive
closer your shadow than on the paper,
and in the rush of blood that lets you live.

We MOVED BACK into the future
and no one understood what we said
and we leapt through the centuries
but no one heard whether we came closer
or further away,

and we could hear what they said
but could not see what they did,
events that were directed
towards some dreamers' plan
in which we knew their next move
without their knowing ours
or why it was we had come
with a host of thoughts from the past.

We were shadows in a dream
and moved back into the future
to express these words
where every word was a fall
out of life, into history.

Who does not grow older,
but wiser like Jacob,
you draw a cloud, and look up.
Who is a calculation
when you do not tally,
what you add subtract and vice versa,
all the elements
in one and the same second
will rise like air and the earth descend
in a deceptive dream in which you are the things you do,
a ladder that you climb,
falls down.

Who will be what you do not see,
not a wonder in the book
without the pages disappearing.
Good night, you said, no promises.

FOR EVERYTHING is found in oblivion
and all that I collect
becomes an awareness of everything
because you are blind, Tiresias
and can count the steps
from the living to the dead
I go to you.

When time runs out
and eyes shut
and the false rings true
questions are never set;
the hum of bees and the flight of birds,
whatever,

but the truth emerged as a poem
as proof of the past,
a lie that could see further
than I wanted to
this is my continuation
my answer, my word;
I spit it out
because you are worth more alive
when the gods dream
and not man.

Morten Øen

~

Norway
translated by David McDuff

overcome I build myths, time's crystal wave, diverse
days' correctness, the dream of inside, low sun, the feeling of
past, like structural elements, loved forth and earlier
seen: Towers of stone and glass. Oceans to disappear in. Forests against
oblivion

I build bridges, corners of the world, all material things. My
mirror-image is: blue eyes, a wrapped-up minute, ceded warmth, and I
get up like a survivor who almost lost his chance
and you say we are bodies, breathing machines, bought time. Floating
falling. misleading

IT IS I OR THE DARKNESS. Experimentally meet over deeper seas
the flight you catch me at time after time

and from the mouth: Like that you lose sleep, sun, loss, but are
more intensely loved

it is here it bleeds. Ineffective in this undone attempt
obeying like neutralities, and hidden in all that is physical

OTHER EVIDENCE EXISTS. Others exist
and are granted to you

inexhaustible body
sand
possible crossing
from lifelessness to reflection
and human
signs

I THINK: the ocean's thermohaline circulation
the weight of the trees on the forest floor

direct answers, temporary solutions

that in this swarm nothing is lost
nothing is forgotten

that from the gate to the stone stairway
it is your back that convinces

several pictures from the same time

Too close to the sun one evening as though it is immortal we are
ruin's attractions, unstoppable like the past, a
lacking call for mercy, or on inborn frequencies of
skill; diverging and processed by others, shaped like
metal, lacking ardor of life or death

TEARS HEARTS in sleep
in realities' attack of intimacy, the spread of city darkness, the steel
of buildings

...circle and you are out of position. That fundamental
vagueness you
explain yourself with, this you have me in

I AM NOT THE LOVER YOU ASKED FOR, that remorse-light gaze
through the winter mirror of the city light, or softer cries
muted year
by year

but like the darkness I yearn into you, gather and
sink just as continuously as ill-timed. As elaborate as
the difference between born and dead

A BLUE JUG filled with water against the light's heat...

movement in the book's shoulder
an outline in your breasts, you who are reading, what do you
    read in this, you
who are her, are you not here

Then you write yourself in all the same
Then we write ourselves in
Then we write ourselves in equally

and it is summer

you consider yourself a visionary
you consider yourself

a different form. A life no one has anything against, that doesn't arise
without further ado

and why this now, so precarious
why these deficiencies in a mirror for eyes

there is something of us here, and in order to confuse
I shut you out

there are songs for lost and lonely. Nothing
forsaken is forsaken

as streetlamps are reflected in water the sky above us is first the
one, then the other

summer then rain. The pavements' curves. Direction which accessible
now

added as real is maybe time sign. This is my name

like: Are swallows lonely
or: This is a flower made of paper

then you make it difficult again

day 1: Enrichment. You are a word
so it tears and tears. My hand against another's, just images
cheek. Mist. 8 mm.

word against word, or

all this just because a romantic setback is exactly
like Old Friends or Child

just as text emerges from text so sound too is a string

we are 12 years old. The child is a stranger's

seen in relation to the landscape's size there are not many places
I have been. No one misses me

not the illusions, but ear-splitting silence is used
as in four three four

one colors. One sits and one stays sitting. One thinks
    something is lacking...
this is how I tell you about us
all over again:
this is how I tell you about us. About summer heat or valley
    floor. The outbreak
of darkness

as Horizon
as Suggested =

your room. Your view

this is how one life lengthens the next. Otherwise it is

sequence:
voices to tell in

and so this is how it has become, I think

there is daylight here (or as close to it as one can get)
dream and hour

I rattle off The Sleepless Nights. Your reality as
more desirable than mine

the same dead end you regret

and when you are here, why point defenselessly backward

                              this under the trees
                                 the white pavilion
                    what ploughed furrows. What a place

what a place

how much can you remember

once I was tall and comely like you
thought as bird/hand

we read our past
from earth to person. No context. All the same

read yourself into this. Once I was almost like you

DUST-YELLOW PLAINS or forest
impending choice where journey is transfer that cannot be
communicated
or presented

stone is not Stone As Burden
writing not approached

burnt paper, salt
earth in this fading light

land without us

PEDRO CARMONA-ALVAREZ

~

NORWAY
TRANSLATED BY INGVILD BURKEY

WE DO PIROUETTES

create scandals   even as it teaches us, tempt
hands and tongue

New York City   1980
        in night clubs *ideas* are exchanged
phone numbers and kisses   favorite books:
Gray's Anatomy, Phantom Engineer
        cigarettes: *Acapulco Gold*   soon
it dawns and you walk along the bank
with her in your hand, in your mouth and we write
each other about this   that she bites, that the one thing
keeping us awake
are dogs, howls   orders for new days, her in
your mouth   everywhere we hear
the whirling, our friends   the electric emperors
of yesterday   asking
and asking   what does fear taste like
(*aluminum*)   and what is the sound
of mercury   (*zimmermann*)

we remember
and we give it a name

I WORK IN THE GARDEN, at night set the alarm
wake up anyway
long before, from the heat, from the sound of bugs, gulls
and trees; indifference is always mirrored in nature
the roots of trees billions of years ago
the animal flayed, surrendering its skin
to a Roman legionary
his sandals and the leather pouch he fills
with coins and herbs
I wash my face, earlier this year
I drained the well and collected spiders
in huge jam jars
this is my room (long ago it was a living room)
this is where I get up
in the middle of the night so I can work
before the heat, before the sun rises and the ocean evaporates
and everything disappears in the haze

certain things happen over night
certain things are more or less simultaneous, in the beginning
image and writing were the same form of expression

WHEN THE EVENTS ATTRACT other, less radiant
sequences on the outskirts of the story
and all the misfortunes and time (writing) emerge
with glassy clarity and precision

When (under the *wings* of language) something unseen develops
over the bodies, a sort of growth
or habit, something we knew even as kids
once when we stood on the outskirts of these very sentences
and a dead dog
by the road (a few feet away)
was the least accidental thing in our lives

We also inherit death, *The Divine Comedy*
and the memory of fire

We do not lack direction
We are not sunburned or lazy
We are not between two or more languages, the place
which belongs to no one

out of weariness you rub your eyes
and a moment later
are surrounded by angels
dust, some other buildings
and next century's most radiant children

VIRGINIA

Virginia, I never finish
I don't sleep anymore, in biology (I think)
there is talk of animals
who during daylight were in constant danger
and therefore developed night vision
black eyes and the sense of hearing, I've made up
my mind from now on
to listen for sirens (in the cities), twigs
stop collecting, photographing
remains, reading novels
I hardly ever dream
anymore of the sister I dream
of having, I lie down
on the red bed, I sleep
standing at first, later
I walk home alone

*

(it's mid-July, suddenly it feels important to let you know
when things happen)
this is the time after a reception, Virginia
can I say that I miss you

*

it's July, I know
that the city and all the birds are part
of a greater work, it's easy
to wish for superpowers, other bodies
Chinese masks and shields (for protection)
I go over the photographs one more time, spread them out on the bed
study the birth marks, a couple of streets
in Managua, Virginia
I don't blame *the narrator*, I want sentences to be true

*

The narrator :   winter,
Virginia through the night   loved   tired
of transparent mouths
The wandering laments, it's called terrain
that which unfolds dispassionately and idly

          let's see: he wanted to learn about leprosy
he wanted to feel in his belly
          the pain at night, later
this fog-like state
          seated facing the garden with eyes
and tongue   reptilian apparatus
          prepared for the infinitely sad stories
of the patients
          on this or the other side of this
or the other war
          the amputations you read about in the papers
the seven or eight
          hundred innocents, the five thousand
with burning hands
          let's see: he desperately wanted to get to know
          a girl named Virginia,
it was her hands
          over his breast, her congenital heart disease
and fear
          of knives and contemporary novels

*

Winter, Virginia through the night. I mention it
by accident, the eleventh of February
I love Picasso, Cortázar, Armani
Listen to the footsteps up the stairs   every night
witnesses impossible transitions
from darkness to light

I've lived in forty cities, I've loved an outlaw,

the perfect bridges and the length of a year

> *The same goddamn streets*
> *The same goddamn food*

Today is my birthday, and some people always go mute
in time, motherfucker

*

Virginia, the man of lead compiles, writes war,
photographs of war   describes the climatic
landscape   Cadiz nights   fire, the sole
repository of *the history of the modern world*
let's see: he intended to drive out of the cities, we remember
the armchair *voltaire* and two diary jottings; one red and one
blue notebook   his wife, we remember Octavia
he was going to hear her again on a beach in Cadiz,
we remember (too often we remember *for* him)
her *Maximus! Maximus! Maximus!*
the pesky writers
and the communist boys

Let's see: he was going to put on his act for seven nights, father
a child with the lightest eyes, whom he calls Pablito
he was going to sleep with her just one more time and write
this sentence just one more time and be graceful just
one more time   *the soothing nights near Cadiz*
and dictionaries

besides, Virginia   he wanted to hear
the song you sing at night
to whoever will listen   if he asks   answer
it's summer, it's summer it's
summer, what we have now   the sin, he wanted to know
why breath and that which strokes
      why something grows steadily toward precision

why it always rains like in books
   without desire, but with infinite patience

there will be other times, the annihilation   other
sentences
parasitical eroticism, everywhere gamblers old swine
drinking   old skin
under the skin of lovers
and Virginia   the hand which stops stroking is
your hand

Centuries ago we died of it
we drowned in rivers, we studied theology, visited
mexico before we traveled back
to europe
to the seventeen year old girls we constantly marry
we bought new clothes and turned our back on the family
forsook our friends, wrote
a small confessional novel, knew juan gris
in paris when he was starving, dying and rotting
in a photograph, compressed all of beethoven's symphonies
into brief progressions of noise
robbed and were hanged
in a photograph, lived alone for thirty four years
before we recovered a lost daughter   we drowned
in cadiz, stopped breathing after four days screaming
in an abandoned mine, for twenty four days and nights we wait
in the cellar of a peasant family
before we are found, we stand with our hands raised
as the bullets rip into the belly heart lungs
we make love to her first soundlessly in the filthy hotel room
we see them through the window, we get dressed
hear them coming up the stairs and put away, on the bedside table
the wedding ring
we were, without doubt, dictators   we confess
guilt, war
was our idea, those we sent to their deaths
the nuns we murdered, the mothers who came looking for their sons
we loved our people, we traveled inland
visited mines and execution squads, rust
and mothers crying, shot screaming my son
goddammit my son

we go out in the morning of the fifteenth of february, we are blown
to pieces in the middle of the street
in mexico city, with our wives and children, we are
senators, vice presidents

we drink coffee in the cafeteria, read plato's dialogues, hear
sirens and something being ripped open
we can stand it only for a few hours
we hear something approaching, the body chimes
against dead empires, the body spitted on a stake
we die of it, the nineteen year old rider
chops off heads
chops off hands
chops off ears, teaches us the words
death and clamor

we are a child that doesn't speak, the child of kings
growing up among monkeys
and stray dogs

we are women who resemble
slaves, are whipped
like slaves

we are the misogynist who desires
his grandmother, his mother
and sister, all
women and animals
of the female sex   centuries ago we froze under the ice
wandered through the streets of santiago
and after thirty five days of heavy drinking
we feel the unstoppable in our lungs
something catches up with us
and by our sister's side
we die of it

POET BIOGRAPHIES

~

Pedro Carmona-Alvarez (Norway), b. 1972, has published three collections of poetry. Born in Chile, he now translates work from Spanish into Norwegian. He writes lyrics and sings for the band *Sister Sonny* and edits the literary magazine *Vagant*.

Didda (Sigurlaug Jónsdóttir) (Iceland), b. 1964, writes rock lyrics as well as lyrics for radio and theater. In addition to authoring several poetry collections and CD's, in 2003 she was awarded the Best Actress in Icelandic Films Prize.

Pär Hansson (Sweden), b. 1970, has taught creative writing in Gothenburg and published three poetry collections. He enjoys a reputation as a stage-poet and is an editor of the poetry leaflet *Gräs* (*Grass*).

Tone Hødnebø (Norway), b. 1962, has published four books of poetry, a book of poetics, *Skamfulle Pompeii* (*Bashful Pompeii*, 2004), and translated Emily Dickinson into Norwegian. She was editor of the literary magazine *Vagant* from 1990-1995. She has been awarded several national literary awards, among them the Norwegian Poetry Award (1998), the Sult Prize (2004), and the Doblong Prize (2005).

Pia Juul (Denmark), b. 1962, has published seven books of poetry, prose, and plays. She has translated the work of Ted Hughes and Michael Cunningham, among others, into Danish, and she has been awarded several national literary awards. These include the Emil Aarestrup Medal (1994), the Limfjordsegnens Literature Prize, the Thøger Larsen Prize, and the Beatrice Prize from the Danish Academy (2000).

Jyrki Kiiskinen (Finland), b. 1963, won the Kalevi Jäntti Prize with his first novel, *Suomies (Bog Man)*. In addition to publishing eight books of poetry and prose, he was the editor-in-chief from 1996 to 2000 of the magazine Books From Finland. He has translated into Finnish poetry originally written in Spanish, French, and English. He was awarded the Dancing Bear Award by the Finnish National Broadcasting Company for the best book of poetry published in 2000.

Jörgen Lind (Sweden), b. 1966, has published five books of poetry. He studied general literature, theology, and creative writing at the Writers' School in Copenhagen and has translated Pia Juul's work into Swedish. He organizes literary events in Gothenburg, where he lives, and edits the poetry leaflet *Gräs (Grass)*.

Morten Øen (Norway), b. 1969, is an art photographer, has published ten books of poetry, and has translated Michael Palmer's work into Norwegian. He was awarded the Oktober Publisher's Prize in 2001. He attended the Writer's School (Bø College) in 1988, where he now teaches poetry and film writing.

Markku Paasonen (Finland), b. 1967, is the former editor-in-chief of the literary magazine *Nuori Voima (Youthful Vigor)*. In addition to publishing four volumes of poetry, he has studied philosophy and theology in Norway, Germany, and Finland. He won the Finnish State Literature Award in 2002.

Lars Mikael Raattamaa (Sweden), b. 1964, is an architect and has published four collections of poetry. He was awarded the Poetry Award by the Swedish National Broadcasting Company in 2001.

Håkan Sandell (Sweden), b. 1962, has published ten volumes of poetry, as well as several books in other genres and translations. He lives in Oslo, Norway, and is one of the main organizers of the Scandinavian retrogardist art movement, which holds much in common with the New Formalism and New Narrative movements in the US.

Helena Sinervo (Finland), b. 1962, is a literary critic, translator, and poet. In addition to publishing five poetry collections and a novel, she has translated the work of Elizabeth Bishop, Yves Bonnefoy, and others into Finnish. Her first novel *Runoilijan talossa* (*In a Poet's House*) won the Finlandia Prize in 2004. She was awarded the Dancing Bear Award by the Finnish National Broadcasting Company for the best book of poetry in 2001.

Lars Skinnebach (Denmark), b. 1973, has published two books of poetry and has had his work included in a book collecting the work of four Danish poets. He in a former editor of *Den blå port* (*The Blue Gate*), a leading Danish literary magazine. He currently lives in Bergen, Norway.

Morten Søndergaard (Denmark), b. 1964, studied creative writing at the Writers' School in Copenhagen and general literature at the University of Copenhagen. In addition to publishing seven books of poetry and prose, he has created "voice experiments" for radio and other media. In 1998, Søndergaard was awarded the Strunge Prize, and in 2003, his poetry collection *Vinci, senere* (*Vinci, later*) was shortlisted for the Nordic Council's Literature Award, the largest and most prestigious award for Nordic literature. He lives in Toscana, Italy.

Nicolaj Stochholm (Denmark), b. 1966, has published four books of poetry. Three of them were republished as the trilogy *Sange fra et ophør* (*Songs from an Ending - collected poems*) in 2000. He has lived in France, Spain, and Ireland for more than 8 years; he currently lives in Copenhagen, Denmark. Some of his national literary awards include The Michael Strunge Prize (1994), the Beatrice Prize from the Danish Academy (2002), and the Emil Aarestrup Medal from the Danish Writers Association (2003).

Anni Sumari (Finland), b. 1965, has published ten books of poetry and short prose, including one travelogue. She has translated the work of Samuel Beckett, Robert Antoni, and Bernardine Evaristo into Finnish and edited anthologies of Finnish poetry. She worked in public relations for seven years and has taught creative writing at Helsinki Critical College. In 1998, she was awarded the Dancing Bear Award by the Finnish National Broadcasting Company for the best book of poetry published that year.

Sigurbjörg Thrastardóttir (Iceland), b. 1973, is a writer and journalist in Reykjavik. Her second book, *Hnattflug* (*Circumnavigation*) was designated the best poetry collection of the season by Icelandic bookshops. Her first novel, *Sólar Saga* (*The Story of the Sun*) won the Tómas Gudmundsson Prize in 2002.